GALBRAITH AND MARKET CAPITALISM

GALBRAITH AND MARKET CAPITALISM

David Reisman

New York University Press. New York *and* London

Library of Congress Cataloging in Publication Data

Reisman, David A
  Galbraith and market capitalism.

  Bibliography: p.
  Includes index.
  1. Galbraith, John Kenneth, 1908–
2. Capitalism. I. Title.
HB119.G33R44   330.12'2   79–9688
ISBN 0–8147–7380–X
ISBN 0–8147–7381–8 pbk.

Printed in Great Britain

Contents

Acknowledgements

The author and publishers wish to thank the following for permission to quote from the works of Professor John Kenneth Galbraith: André Deutsch Ltd and Houghton Mifflin Company for extracts from *The Affluent Society*, © 1958, 1969, 1976, *Economics and the Public Purpose* © 1973, *Economics, Peace and Laughter* © 1971, and *The New Industrial State* © 1967, 1971; M. E. Sharpe, Inc. for an extract from *American Capitalism*, © 1952, 1956, 1980.

1 Introduction: Galbraith and Market Capitalism

Galbraith is witty, provocative, stimulating, intelligent, unorthodox, outspoken and eminently readable. He is also vague, repetitious, arrogant, mercenary, journalistic, dogmatic and an élitist snob. Above all he is important, challenging, controversial and confusing. The present book is intended as an attempt to make sense of the complexities of Galbraith's work and to provide a tentative assessment of a social critic frighteningly easy to read and tantalisingly difficult to understand. The present book is also concerned with the theory and practice of market capitalism, for it is that which occupies the centre of the stage in the epic drama of the Galbraithian system.

John Kenneth Galbraith believes that men orientate themselves not to phenomena but to the images of those phenomena which they have formed in their minds; and that ideologies and belief-systems are of particular value as a map in the somewhat forbidding world of economic and social reality. It so happens, however, that, because in explanations of social phenomena 'all tactical advantage is with the acceptable', [1] that consensus of opinion which is generally taken as true without further proof is frequently out of date. The conventional wisdom ensures continuity in social thought and action; but, since events move more quickly than ideas, it also causes theory to lag behind practice. The conventional wisdom is thus conservative of past convictions at the cost of grossly distorted perceptions concerning contemporary realities. It is a bad map; and seldom more evidently so, in Galbraith's view, than in the case of the ideology of market capitalism. This obsolete map around the complexities of modern economic and social phenomena is seen by Galbraith to possess the following features:

(a) *The firm*

The ideology of market capitalism argues in terms of perfect competition (a situation where there are a large number of buyers and sellers, each a price-taker rather than a price-setter, none with the power to influence the prices at which he trades his outputs or the costs which he incurs to purchase his inputs) and rational profit-maximisation (a situation where producers take maximum return to capital as their objective on the analogy with a self-made, self-reliant, hard-working entrepreneur who, in a market environment characterised by survival only of the fittest, could afford to have no other).

Such a system of atomistic competition and free enterprise capitalism automatically and invisibly ensures the optimal allocation of resources and is thus economically efficient. The system is in addition socially efficient; for it provides an incentive to the producer to supply those goods and services for which there is an effective demand—those goods and services, in other words, which consumers happen to want to buy.

(b) *The consumer*

The ideology of market capitalism argues in terms of consumer sovereignty and assumes that buyers make ultimate decisions while sellers only execute the will of their masters. The invisible hand of the market mechanism is held to convey to the firm information about the innate and authentic desires of the consumerhood; and, by ensuring that firms compete with one another for the attentions of the prudent shopper, to guarantee fair prices, sound workmanship and adequate choice.

The purchaser is the original locus of power and initiative in this model; and hence choice is taken to mean individual choice, responsibility to signify individual responsibility. If, in this model, the goods demanded turn out to be lethal or environmentally deleterious, then the consumer is to blame and not the producer; for empirically observable preference-patterns, it is argued, merely reflect 'the public choice. If people are abused, it is because they choose self-abuse. If economic behaviour seems on occasion insane, it is because people are insane.'[2] Tolerance and a belief in human dignity then give the economic system its teleology, its sense of purpose: 'The best economic system is the one that supplies the most of what people most want.'[3] Allocation and growth become central issues in a world where value-free observation and non-judgemental induction demonstrate that man (man, at least, in market capitalist society) is not ascetic but acquisitive and materialistic in his outlook, and suggest that an expanded supply of scarce goods and services intended to satisfy apparently insatiable appetites may be taken as a legitimate indicator of social achievement.

(c) The government

The ideology of market capitalism argues in terms of political *laissez-faire* and recommends that, since the most efficient allocation of resources and the most sensitive response to consumer demands can only be brought about through the free operation of the market mechanism, the State should confine its interference in economic and social life to the performance of crucial functions either indispensably complementary to private activity (such as the guarantee of law and order, defence and the enforcement of contracts) or indispensably regulatory of it (such as the inspection of weights and measures and the control of dangerous drugs). Ideology notes that 'in a state of bliss, there is no need for a Ministry of Bliss'[4]; records how often civil servants tend to be apathetic, misguided and inefficient, rulers to be corrupt, tyrannical and ill-inspired; and warns that, just as individual freedom is symbiotically associated with freedom of enterprise, so authoritarianism and totalitarianism are the inevitable concomitants of any socialist system which directs the allocation of resources and distorts the pattern of authentic individual desires. Ideology in the past has taught that 'to be for new schools, against air pollution or in favour of stronger zoning laws was to be in support of the first awful step down the slippery path to communism',[5] and is today no less hostile to these and other forms of Big Brotherism in social life.

Any understanding of the importance of Galbraith's contribution to contemporary thought reduces itself to an understanding of why Galbraith believes the ideology of market capitalism to be increasingly incapable of explaining economic and social reality as it exists today, and thus to be increasingly inappropriate as a basis for policy recommendations. Galbraith's case against the possessively individualistic fictions of late utilitarianism is by no means a simple one, but the main characteristics are the following:

(a) The firm

The mature corporation, unlike the small perfect competitor, deploys giant units of capital in technology-intensive lines of production, has decision-horizons that stretch far into a potentially uncertain future, and is hence dependent on the predictability of supply and demand conditions yet to come. Fortunately for the mature corporation, however, planning goes beyond mere forecasting and involves the active exercise of economic power to mould and shape future economic and social conditions by means of techniques such as inter-firm contracts, vertical and horizontal integration, concord with the trade unions, symbiosis with the State, and manipulation of consumer demand. In the world of today, in other words, large organisations have considerable power to bend the community to their will; and it might even be asserted that 'people increasingly served the convenience of these organizations which were meant to serve *them*'.[6]

Probing deeply within the giant corporation discover the true identity of our faceless masters, we find that ownership is now separate from management and management from control, and ultimately isolate the locus of power and initiative in the technostructure, that body of scientists, engineers, economists, accountants and other specialists which collectively makes decisions and plans the future development of the firm. In such a post-capitalist environment (and it accounts for as much as half of output in the private sector), profit-maximisation has ceased to be a primary consideration; and, so long as the supply of profits is adequate to pacify shareholders and generate sufficient internal funds for reinvestment, the team is free to pursue goals of its own (notably job-satisfaction, security and growth) more attractive than profits to the boffin on a salary.

(b) The consumer

In a world of manipulation and persuasion by means of advertising and salesmanship, the myth of consumer sovereignty must be abandoned and the underlying reality accepted that the citizen today demands an increasing quantity of goods and services primarily because it suits the objectives of large organisations for him to do so. Clearly, however, in an era when the cost of manufacturing desires rivals the cost of manufacturing commodities and when power has devolved from buyer to seller, want-satisfaction can no longer be taken as a legitimate justification for economic growth; for, and quite apart from distortions induced by the sales-strategies of the powerful, the fact is that consumers can become satiated with affluence and are indeed already becoming so.

(c) The government

The modern economy is rich in privately provided consumables (such as electric toothbrushes and colour televisions); the modern society is poor in collectively provided services (such as support to social welfare, including education, low-cost housing and public transport; support to the arts, to small firms so that they might survive in a world dominated by the large and the powerful, to giant corporations so that they might conduct research and development in new and risky areas of technological advance; control of inflation via a prices and incomes policy which has the subsidiary objective of redistributing the national income towards the low-paid, who ought also to benefit from minimum wage legislation); the modern polity has a duty to fill the gap when it comes to support and regulation and thus to ensure a balanced society rather than one subservient to the goals of the giant corporation. A move towards collective consumption is a desirable thing in its own right, but it is in any case truly thrust upon us; for in area after area of modern life, 'as a purely technical matter, there is no alternative to public management'.[7] It is not clear what Great Man first laid down the laws of nature. There can be no doubt, however, that he was a democratic socialist.

If the modern State is to provide more services and fulfill more functions, then the administration of the State itself must be reformed. Specifically, power must be transferred from organisationally imprisoned bureaucrats to socially accountable politicians, and among politicians from conservatives (committed to obsolete ideological relics and the intellectual artifacts of the past) to radicals (aware that the horse has become the rider in temporary defiance of the momentum inherent in matter); and this in turn presupposes the ideological emancipation of the electorate, a service to be performed not by the guild of economists (whose minds are unfortunately so befuddled by the outdated theology of market capitalism that they are no longer competent to reveal truth or uncover reality) but most significantly by the educational and scientific estate (whose minds are fresh and open and who see clearly what is happening in the world around them). Each group has its allies (the former group is cheered on by organisation men, the rich, and by lazy thinkers who do not sense the emergence of an intellectual vacuum; while the latter group is supported by technocrats in lame-duck corporations, consumers aware of manipulation and citizens concerned by links of interest forged between corporate capitalism and defence-related bureaucracies), but it is the latter which will win: it, after all, has the logic of circumstances on its side, and thus successfully 'illuminates the anxieties of the time'.[8]

The millenium is inevitable; but nonetheless 'one can always try to advance the inevitable'.[9] Galbraith has tried to do this and has succeeded in consequence in stimulating more popular discussion of economic, social and political questions than has any other intellectual of his generation. Popular discussion is always a good thing; and even those who disagree with his specific hypotheses or question either the inevitability or the desirability of the socialist society which he anticipates are immensely in his debt for having lit up the sky.

2 The Technostructure and its Goals

The reliance on advanced technology and the employment of large quantities of capital in the modern corporation have, by putting a premium on skill and knowledge, given rise to a new dominant élite, the technostructure. In Section I of this chapter we will examine the nature of this new class, in Section II consider its goals and in Section III investigate the position of the old-style capitalist in the new-style scheme of things. In Section IV we will attempt an evaluation of Galbraith's views on the technostructure and its goals.

I THE TECHNOSTRUCTURE

Galbraith believes that power and prestige derive from the ownership of a scarce factor of production (i.e. an input with a high inelasticity of supply at the margin). In feudalism this scarce factor was land. In early capitalism it was physical capital. In modern capitalism it is specialised expertise, both technological and organisational. This being the case, it is no surprise to find in the new industrial state that particular esteem is attracted not by the financier, the capitalist, the landowner or the manual labourer but by the research chemist and the economic forecaster (as indeed by the workers in the education industry who turn out the strategic input).

Expertise alone is not enough, however. Modern technology is sophisticated and necessitates such division and subdivision of function that each expert ends up knowing a lot about a little. Consequently, since complex processes require ability, intelligence, knowledge and intuition beyond that in the possession of any one individual, decision-making becomes collective. In the modern corporation, information is shared among the members of a large group of anonymous specialists, a balanced team of product

7

planners, engineers, advertising and sales executives, market re-
searchers, public relations men, scientists, lobbyists, accountants,
economists and other highly skilled experts. Understandably, no
one individual has more than a fraction of the experience of
production, judgement of design, information about marketing,
skill in influencing government necessary to form a complete
picture and reach a reasonable conclusion, and therefore decisions
are made by committees as the result of the interplay of ideas and
the synthesis of combined insights. Organised and collective
intelligence alone, in the form of the technostructure, has the
information and ability to make meaningful decisions. The success
of the modern corporation is proof that 'committee' need not be
synonymous with inaction, and testifies to the efficiency of the group
mind.

This analysis implies that the Weberian conception of bureaucracy in terms of 'a formal structure of command' is largely obsolete
and 'must be abandoned'.[1] The technostructure is a pooling
arrangement, and one man's decision simply cannot be referred to
his superior in the hierarchy: only a superior committee can
evaluate the work of an inferior, and such control from without is
seldom likely to be found.

The technostructure, like any bureaucracy, is a self-perpetuating
body, and the reason is its 'synthetic personality'.[2] Genius is in
unpredictable supply and hence nowadays 'instead of genius, the
large corporation makes use of the combined efforts of many men of
specialized but not remarkable ability. It substitutes organization
for exceptional individual qualifications'.[3] Individuals come and go
but the boxes they fill in the scheme of functional interdependence
go on unchanged. In contrast to that of the classical owner-
entrepreneur, the death, retirement or resignation of the most gifted
sales executive or most brilliant research chemist (or even of the
company president himself) passes unnoticed by outsiders and has
no influence on the image or financial standing of the corporation.
What matters most is continuity of structure.

The organisation man tends quite naturally to develop a
particular kind of personality, and this results from his job-function.
He learns not to be competitive but to be cooperative, and comes to
respect the dependence of each upon all in coordinated group
action. He learns to recognise that he is a mere cell in a larger
organism whose accomplishments are 'more than the sum of
isolated individual contributions'.[4] He learns to submerge his

personality in that of the group: an entrepreneur can afford to be fiercely individualistic, but a technocrat must adapt to others.

Perhaps such a conformist way of life is deplorable; but, after all, the organisation man does commit himself voluntarily and can escape if he so desires. Moreover, the problem must be kept in perspective: the organisation man is a 'type', but 'the competitive market also has its type. It is not clear that the wary, uncompassionate, self-regarding, wit-matching rug dealer, in whom both deviousness and cupidity may have been as often rewarded as penalized, would have been kept in the Temple while the organization man was expelled.'[5] Finally, it is important to remember that, despite the emergence of a group personality, there is nonetheless still scope for individuality within the technostructure. After all, much exchange of information and opinion is by word of mouth, through discussion; and here a particularly persuasive debater can considerably influence others quite independent of his nominal position in the formal structure. In a world of specialists and group decisions, effective participation in decision-making may actually be more a function of personality than in a hierarchy with a less diffuse locus of power.

In the modern corporation, specialists make decisions, while non-participant managers and boards of directors merely ratify them: 'It will be evident that nearly all powers – initiation, character of development, rejection or acceptance – are exercised deep in the company. . . . Effective power of decision is lodged deeply in the technical, planning and other specialized staff.'[6] The managerial revolution has been superseded by the technocratic revolution, and nowadays 'it is not the managers who decide'.[7] The technostructure quite understandably fears intervention even from its nominal superiors, since managers and directors are not part of group decision-making processes. The bosses, however, appear content to leave decisions on products, prices and policy to the technostructure, whose collective intelligence they cannot hope to evaluate or challenge. A revised interpretation must naturally be given to the master–servant relationship in our brave new world where it is the latter who give the orders.

II THE GOALS OF THE TECHNOSTRUCTURE

The elementary textbook explanation of the goals of the firm is simple: the firm seeks to maximise its profits. Small perfect competitor and huge monopolist alike are assumed subject to this unique incentive, which has two great advantages: first, it makes models determinate and subject to mathematical presentation with considerable rigour; and, second, it has the beneficient philosophical property of demonstrating that avarice and ambition can benefit the whole community via the market mechanism.

For the technostructure, however, the goal of profit-maximisation is eminently marginal since experts are rewarded by fixed salaries which do not vary with the profits of the firm. It is hence unlikely that the corporation where power to decide is firmly in the hands of the technostructure (the 'mature' corporation) will be outstandingly profitable, and empirical evidence is available to support this hypothesis: 'Monsen, Chiu and Cooley for the twelve years 1952 through 1963 have compared the earnings of large firms in which there is full management (i.e. technostructure) control with those in which there is substantial ownership interest. The return on invested capital for the management-controlled firms was substantially and consistently lower.'[8]

The technostructure has goals of its own; and by what Galbraith calls the 'Principle of Consistency' is able to impose them on the giant corporation and on society as a whole. Nowadays society serves the corporation and the corporation serves the technostructure. This being the case, it is important to discover exactly what goals the specialists set themselves, as a preliminary to deciding whether the modern corporation is 'soulful' and serves broad social ends, or at the very least to deciding whether private vices really are public virtues. Galbraith identifies these goals as being three in number: job satisfaction, security and growth. The goals are at least conceptually distinct and it will be useful to examine each in turn:

(a) Job satisfaction

Technocrats welcome the opportunity to express their technical virtuosity, and hence they tend to neglect those consumer-preferences whose satisfaction does not present much of a technical challenge in order to concentrate on the development of products and processes where there is maximum scope for innovation.

Technocrats, moreover, like to feel that they and their corporation are significantly serving the public interest. This sensation, however, is apparently not difficult to acquire: a man 'will normally think that the goals he seeks have social purpose' since people 'have a well-remarked capacity to attach high social purpose to whatever – more scientific research, better zoning laws, manufacture of . . . lethal weapons . . . – serves their personal interest.'[9] Such a capacity does not inspire confidence; and one in particular tends to suspect the philosophical competence and moral discrimination of a specialist who attributes social purpose to 'scientific research' and 'lethal weapons' alike, depending on his 'personal interest'.

(b) Security

Businessmen in the mature corporation often allege that they are as individualistic, aggressive and competitive as the classical entrepreneur; but this is largely romanticisation. The fact is that executive life is highly secure: 'In 1970, a study of the chief executives of 250 among the 500 largest business firms showed that nearly two thirds had joined their present company before 1950 and another 9 per cent before 1956. Of the executives of the very largest industrial and retail firms – those with sales of over a billion dollars – three out of four had been with their companies for more than twenty years.'[10] This security is greatly welcomed by businessmen: no one, understandably enough, likes to lose his job.

Technocrats, too, and especially where they work in committees, enjoy considerable security of employment. They form, after all, the collective brain of the corporation and thus represent within limits a fixed cost to their paymasters (an overhead likely to prove expensive in view of their numbers and generous remuneration). Clearly, the contraction of the technostructure is a calamity to be estimated not just in terms of loss of jobs but also in terms of loss of key specialists from the group and impaired efficiency of those who remain. The technostructure is anxious to keep the team together in so far as minimum size is a precondition for viability, and it greatly fears the dismissal of any of its members.

The technostructure is no less concerned with its autonomy, no less anxious to prevent poorly informed outsiders from interfering in a process of collegial decision-making that ought to be confined to well-informed experts. Such interference is threatening both to the decisions themselves and to the power of the technostructure. The enemies of the technostructure's autonomy are the shareholders, the creditors of the firm (such as banks), the labour force (usually via the unions), the government; and accordingly much of the technostructure's strategy is devoted to neutralising these and other possible sources of outside intervention.

(c) Growth

The technostructure has an affirmative as well as a protective purpose – namely rapid growth of the corporation it serves. The reasons for this affirmative purpose are not hard to find.

First, rapid growth increases the prestige of the firm (especially where that growth is associated with technological progress and innovation, a supremely prestigious activity), and this in turn increases the derived prestige of its personnel. Growth is 'good public relations' since the large and growing firm attracts more applause than the small and static one in a world where rate of expansion, not rate of profit, is the index of success.

Seen from the point of view of the insider, the success of the organisation reflects favourably on its servants. In the late nineteenth century prestige was associated with successful entrepreneurship; in the late twentieth century it is not associated with individuals at all, and two businessmen size each other up by the medium of the question 'Who are you with?' As Galbraith puts it, 'esteem is associated with corporations'.[11] The dynamic corporation is a status symbol and lends a 'rich gloss of reputability' to its servants: 'The men who guide the modern corporation, including the financial, legal, technical, advertising, and other sacerdotal authorities in corporate function, are the most respectable, affluent, and prestigious members of the national community. They are the Establishment. Their interest tends to become the public interest.'[12]

In a world of institutions, 'pre-eminently the organization man is sustained by organization'.[13] The tendency for the individual to bask in the reflected glory of the body that employs him even obtains in the case of the university professor: 'A university, in our society, acts as a prop to the individual. As a member of the university community, he is much; divorced from it, he is on his own and maybe much less.'[14]

Second, growth of sales often rewards those men directly who are most responsible for it. Despite the collegial nature of decision-making, it is evidently still possible for an outstanding individual to get on. For example: 'The marketing man who successfully persuades the public to buy some abnormally improbable artifact will, in consequence, be in charge of the resulting larger marketing operation. He promotes himself along with the product.'[15]

Third, corporate growth means both expansion of the techno-structure and improved promotion possibilities for all. The techno-structure naturally welcomes the growth of the team via the addition of new members, partly because expansion is the best protection against contraction. This implies that there is no organisational constraint on growth, 'no set upper limit to the size of the firm'[16]: collective decision-making means that the maximum size of the enterprise is not constrained by the energy and intellect of a single chief. Moreover, in a growing corporation there is not a morbid fascination with dead men's shoes, nor a premium on aggression against one's superiors, nor a fear of aggression against oneself. In a static organisation an individual's advancement depends on the death or retirement of the person above him in the hierarchy (or on his ability to displace such a person), while in a dynamic organisation new jobs are being created and promotion ceases to be a zero-sum game (where my gain is your loss and vice versa). As a corollary, cooperation and organic solidarity among members of the team is maximised once competition between them is minimised.

Fourth, the growth of the corporation increases its power, and such power may be sought both as an end in itself and for the security it confers. The decision-makers of the large firm influence not only the lives of the people working under their direction but the broad social environment as well: 'With size goes the ultimate responsibility for the decisions affecting the largest number of employees, over prices that affect the largest number of customers, over investment policies which work the greatest change in the income, livelihood, or landscape of the community.'[17]

The larger the firm, the more it will be able to influence crucial parameters such as prices and costs and thus to ensure its own security. The technostructure is, however, here involved in a dilemma: security presupposes growth, but growth means change and hence uncertainty. Moreover, change is inextricably linked to the objective of job satisfaction (since it is in a dynamic organisation that the expert has maximum challenge and maximum opportunity to exercise his intelligence and ingenuity). Goals are interdependent, possibly contradictory, and the most one can say by way of prediction is that the technostructure is likely to err on the side of caution by pursuing growth while avoiding unnecessary risks.

Spectacular earnings of the corporation, after all, add proportionately less to the welfare of the technocrats than spectacular
failures detract from it: 'Loss can destroy the technostructure; high
revenues accrue to others.'[18] Even this prediction must be modified,
however: each technostructure has three goals, and the precise
balance between them will vary as between firms.

Fifth, the growth of the corporation means higher earnings for the
employee. Galbraith is adamant that the technocrat is not averse
to good pay: 'Pecuniary compensation is an extremely important
stimulus to individual members of the technostructure up to a point.
If they are not paid this acceptable and expected salary, they will
not work.'[19] At the same time, however, just as the rate of profit
beyond a threshold minimum is no longer of prime importance to
the corporation, so the rate of pay beyond a given level has ceased to
be of prime importance to the technocrat. At least in the large
corporations, 'pecuniary compensation, as an explanation of effort,
has now a relatively much diminished role'.[20]

The reason for the revised pattern of motivation is that the
technostructure nowadays tends to identify with the corporation
and also considers itself able to adapt corporate purpose to
participant's preference. To a significant extent the corporation
allows the individual to express his creativity (say, through
technological virtuosity) and satisfy many of his psychological needs
(say, through the service of an assumed social purpose). Moreover,
scientists and engineers (whether in universities or private enterprise) have professional pride, which makes them perform well
simply out of love of a job well done. Also, because groups make
decisions, a member of the technostructure does not feel alienated,
powerless or lacking in responsibility.

It is hence highly probable that the high earnings of the
technostructure are largely a by-product of the ability in an
expanding organisation of an able man to win early promotion and
substantial responsibility; and that the technocrat does not seek
advancement merely or even principally with material reward in
mind. The fact remains, however, that material reward, even if
secondary, is still considerable. The reason here is power position
rather than productivity, since, in a world of administered pay
scales and the career structure, it is the men at the top who decide
what each box in the hierarchy ought to receive. As for the chief
executives themselves, pay is completely divorced from performance: 'The salary of the chief executive of the large corporation is

not a market reward for achievement. It is much more in the nature of a thoughtful personal gesture by the individual to himself.'[21]

Pecuniary motivation is, however, more important the further one moves out from the nucleus of the mature corporation that is represented by the managers and the technostructure. Galbraith suggests that the modern large organisation can best be visualised not as a hierarchy of command but as a series of concentric circles, where influence moves out from the centre, not principally down from the top. At the centre of the corporation are the men most likely to regard their work as self-expression, least likely to find their tasks boring, their position insecure, their function primarily to enrich others. In the more distant concentric circles (say, among the unskilled manual labourers) are the malintegrated. Here alienation from the goals of the firm is most likely to be found, effort most likely to be a function of financial incentive. Fortunately, the problem of the malintegrated is not an excessively serious one. Many manual workers do identify with their firm and bask in its prestige, and such a feeling of well-being is heightened where work is comparatively interesting and tenure relatively secure. Trades unions give the worker the opportunity to participate and thus strengthen his sense of integration, while upgrading simultaneously increases the white-collar component in production. Thus, however alienated the production worker may feel, his motivation is seldom if ever as purely pecuniary as is the case with the shareholder, the creature most removed from the attitudes typical of the technostructure.

III THE POSITION OF THE CAPITALIST

The corporate form of ownership results from the need for great quantities of capital. It also represents the 'euthanasia of stock-holder power'[22]: the need to raise more and more finance by share-issues over time (coupled with the break-up of great fortunes due to factors such as philanthropy, inheritance, divorce or death duties) diversifies shareholdings and reduces the power of any individual capitalist. Most shareholders in any case are not only powerless and faceless but also remote from and uninterested in their corporation. They vote their proxies, collect their dividends, and (being totally lacking in a sense of loyalty to or identification with the firm) prefer to sell out rather than (probably ineffectually) challenge the decision-makers.

The function of the owner has thus today become one of ritualistic approbation of decisions already taken by others. This is *de facto* disenfranchisement: the shareholder can vote but his vote is 'valueless'[23] and his power 'nil'.[24] Such disenfranchisement turns out to be relative rather than total, however, as Galbraith notes three cases in which the capitalist might intervene in the running of his corporation:

The first is a shareholders' revolt. This is most likely to occur when the corporation is doing badly (paying low dividends or possibly making losses) and is for that reason alone exceptional in view of the generally good performance of the large firm: 'Big corporations almost never lose money. From 1954 through 1969, there was only one year in which as many as three of the hundred largest industrial corporations lost money.'[25] Moreover, shareholders would, even in such a situation, think twice before acting: the voting out of one set of executives means the voting in of another, and the known evil may be preferable to the unknown. For similar reasons, a take-over bid is not a real threat even to the management of a low-dividend corporation: 'The danger of involuntary takeover is negligible in the management calculations of the large firm and diminishes with growth and dispersal of stock ownership.'[26]

The second is the menace of intervention from institutional investors such as insurance companies or pension funds, which do after all hold substantial portfolios of shares. But here again the danger is minimal: they tend to be passive in practice, and to diversify holdings to such an extent that events in one corporation do not affect them excessively.

The third is the threat which arises when a dominant percentage of shares is in a few hands. In particular, in some of the older corporations the founder's family may still hold a large proportion of stock, and may also occupy crucial posts on the board of directors or in the managerial hierarchy and technostructure. Such families (the obvious examples in the United States context are the Dupont, Ford, Firestone and Rockefeller clans) are eminently well-placed to defend their own interests and the interests of other shareholders as well. The problem must, however, be seen in perspective: founding families are a rarity, and the growth of the corporation will in any case render their blocs of shares percentagewise less significant. This latter development is to be welcomed in the interests of economic democracy and also because it neutralises an important threat to the autonomy of the corporate technostructure.

The three sources of outside intervention are or are becoming insignificant. In normal circumstances the owners are passive, and power to run the mature corporation devolves to the technocrats who make decisions and to the managers and directors who passively ratify them. Such independent exercise of power by the specialist is highly valued by him. The same forces which produce the separation of ownership from control also generate the techno-structure, and these two events must be conjoint, since uninformed intervention in decision-making is always damaging. Knowledge in the new industrial state is so complex that group decision-making is indispensable, and an owner, without being a full-time member of the team, simply does not have adequate information and expertise intelligently to influence company policy. Besides that, there is a potential conflict of interest: owners value maximum profits while technocrats have other goals than maximising returns in which they do not share.

The number and complexity of decisions increase with the size of the corporation – so, fortunately for the technostructure, does the independence of skilled specialists from interested but ignorant owners. The result is that the modern corporate economy comes to depend on a dangerous fiction: the continuing pretence that the owners have power means that the technostructure has power without responsibility.

If the large corporation is dependent more on the passivity of the shareholder than on his activity, the question must arise as to his function. Here Galbraith paints a depressing picture of inaction, of demand without supply: to him, the shareholder is 'a passive and functionless figure, remarkable only in his capacity to share, without effort or even without appreciable risk, in the gains from the growth by which the technostructure measures its success. No grant of feudal privilege has ever equalled, for effortless return, that of the grandparent who bought and endowed his descendants with a thousand shares of General Motors, General Electric or I.B.M.'[27]

Reference to 'effortless return' accruing to a 'passive and functionless figure' might suggest to some more than simply the 'euthanasia of stockholder power', namely the 'euthanasia of stockholder property' itself. It would appear that dividends are as 'non-functional' as the revenues of the landlord in a developing country, whose income is related not to services rendered but to his power as a member of the ruling élite[28]; and Galbraith makes no secret of his view that, in many developing countries, 'there can be no effective design for economic development . . . which does not disestablish the non-functional groups – which does not separate them from political power and, *pari passu*, reduce or eliminate their claim on income. This solution applies equally whether power derives from land, other hierarchical wealth, the Army, the non-functional bureaucracy or some coalition of these.'[29] A similar case could easily be made out for the expropriation of the American shareholder. Galbraith, however, for a considerable period of time chose not to pursue too far the question of what to do, in industrial states, with functionless men who reap where they never sowed.

IV EVALUATION

We are now in a position to evaluate Galbraith's views on the technostructure and its goals:

(a) *The technostructure*

Galbraith alleges that prestige in the new industrial state is most closely associated with the unique scarce factor of skill, but it is by no means clear that this is so. It is by no means certain that the sales executive enjoys prestige because of his glamorous job (which to many probably appears the epitome of corporate treadmilldom) rather than because of the high income it affords him, which in turn allows him (and his wife) to dress well, live in an expensive house in a fashionable suburb, travel in an elegant if not wholly functional car, and in general enjoy the status-symbols associated with wealth. Put differently, the problem is this: what a man earns and spends might be more a source of esteem than the job at which he is employed. An old-style capitalist living off the returns on his investments may have the same income as a modern technocrat living off his salary. The two men may have an identical style of life, and it may be very difficult in practice to say who has more standing in the society and who has less.

As to Galbraith's view that the technostructure makes decisions and nominal managers merely 'give the equivalent of the royal assent',[30] this picture of individual business leaders as powerless, ceremonial figures is highly questionable. It is, after all, the managers who appoint, dismiss and reassign the members of the technostructure, and who thus can bias its composition in one direction or another. It is the managers, moreover, who select the problems for study by the technostructure[31] and who evaluate the evidence provided by the specialists in the light of company policy. This is necessary since the technostructure does not typically give a simple yes/no answer but rather spells out the spectrum of choices open to management (normally, the alternative means that could be used to attain a particular end). This leaves managers free to make the final choice, or indeed to throw out the entire problem and refer another to the technocrats for their study and specialist advice.

Furthermore, managers coordinate the decisions and activities of many groups of experts, and see to it that their activities are consistent with one another. The fact is that the large firm is unlikely to have one technostructure but many, not just because it is multi-product and multi-market, but because each kind of specialist decision requires a different kind of specialist committee. Managers themselves are usually highly skilled – possibly in accountancy, law or even engineering, but certainly in business administration itself – and are likely to play an active part in this network of interlocking technostructures (even if on marketing and finance rather than on chemistry panels). Moreover, not only do managers participate in and coordinate the work of committees, they ensure a hierarchy of objectives because of which pure technocrats are unlikely to be able to impose purely technocratic goals on the firm: managers are unlikely to accord the same importance to product-development for its own sake as they would to, say, aggressive marketing. In any case, even where the technostructure is called upon to advise, the policy decisions they are *least* likely to be able to influence are those concerning the objectives of the firm; and it is impossible not to conclude that managers remain free to set the goals of the corporation. There is, of course, no evidence that technocrats even want to become decision-makers. Galbraith himself makes clear the eagerness of the technostructure to accept objectives from without and even attribute 'high social purpose' to them.

There is hence no reason to think that the locus of power has shifted from management to technostructure or that the techno-cratic has negated the managerial revolution. Even today there is often in business a powerful manager near or at the apex of the corporate hierarchy who can exert his personal influence on the policy of the whole enterprise. Naturally it is easier to recognise the impact of an individual genius on the corporation he himself is creating than to identify the remarkable business leader in an existing and bureaucratised concern; but it is an exaggeration to say, as Galbraith does, that 'the men who now head the great corporations are unknown'.[32] Exceptional individuals do exist, and some investors in their portfolio-policies actually back leaders of talent rather than simply groups or companies.

The same principle applies in the case of financial corporations. It is a red herring to argue that surplus capital leads to inferior prestige: there is no reason to suppose either that social admiration is necessarily attracted by a scarce input nor even that capital is nowadays abundant (many small firms, if not the giants of the planning system, still complain of punitive rates of interest and a capital famine). In general, there is no reason to suppose that a bank is less prestigious than an oil company, or that an outstanding executive will attract less prestige in the one than in the other. Even in the banking industry, the names of exceptional whizz-kids do become known; and their personal magnetism appears to be even greater in the case of non-bank financial intermediaries. It is not impossible to conceive of a celebrated financier (a modern J. P. Morgan) beavering away within the corporate framework of, say, a unit trust.

(b)　The goals of the technostructure

Galbraith's presentation of the personal and private goals of the new specialist élite in terms of job satisfaction, security and growth is ingenious. It is, however, open to attack on several grounds.

First, the growth of the firm is necessary for the technostructure to demonstrate its technical prowess; for its security and independence; and for any improvement in its promotion prospects, power, prestige and pay. But growth must be financed, and where that finance comes chiefly out of retained earnings high profits may in considerable measure be the precondition for rapid growth. The technostructure, in other words, would be foolish to expand sales of a given product excessively: by flooding the market for a good and thereby forcing down its price, it might actually reduce the pool of profits at its disposal for reinvestment and thus both undermine its security and retard its ultimate growth-rate.

This is not to say that the orthodox goal of profit-maximisation and the Galbraithian aim of rapid growth are equivalent. It is, however, true that a theory which predicts corporate policy on the assumption of profit-maximisation may still yield good results despite reliance on behavioural assumptions which Galbraith would regard as outdated and false, precisely because profits are implicitly so necessary for the explicit aims of the technostructure. Galbraith does not appear to recognise that a sacrifice in profitability may mean a sacrifice in growth of sales or in the security of the specialists, and that the pursuit of sales presupposes some prior pursuit of profits (at least to a firm which seeks to guard its autonomy by avoiding outside borrowing). Financial returns may not be the ultimate end for the technocrat in the way that they are for the shareholder, but they are still a very important means to some superior end.

Second, the mature corporation in an imperfect market structure is in a curiously ambiguous position which Galbraith neglects to mention. On the one hand, since it is an imperfect competitor, we would expect some restriction of sales and some increase in price. On the other hand, since it is, according to Galbraith, subject to the goals of the technostructure rather than those of the capitalists, we would expect some expansion of sales and presumably some reduction in price. In such a situation, in other words, the growth-oriented specialist decision-maker might cause the powerful firm to overcome its bias towards abnormally high profits at the cost of abnormally low output; and the final position in terms of prices and quantities could well resemble the solution we would have expected in the paradise of perfect competition. Here, in terms of results (even if not in terms of motivation) the economic system would appear to be retrogressing towards that very ideal of competitive market capitalism which Galbraith believes to be a thing of the past. In terms of results, the system would appear to behave *as if* profits were being maximised in conditions of perfect competition. This socially beneficial – if totally unintended – aspect of the modern technostructure's growth-motive has been stressed by Professor Meade.[33]

Third, it is by no means certain that a high growth-rate of the firm actually increases its prestige more than a high profit-rate would have done. Should a high return on capital be the true source of corporate prestige, the managers (and even enlightened technocrats) might deliberately choose, in the interests of status, not to go for growth. Alternatively, they might recognise that growth means more pay and promotion for themselves, more chance to purchase expensive status-symbols and thus more personal prestige. In such a situation they might maximise personal prestige at the expense of corporate prestige, or attempt a balance between the two sources of prestige by expanding sales at the margin slightly beyond the optimum profits point while simultaneously paring the overshoot to the bare minimum.

Fourth, it is doubtful that technological virtuosity is an independent goal of the mature corporation. As Robin Marris has put it:

> The conclusion that the corporations will not undertake, for example, low-cost housing development because this provides no outlet for technical virtuosity implies both that the difficulty could be overcome if a suitable technical challenge in industrial housing development could be provided and conversely that the mere provision of cash to subsidize rents would not overcome it. Here, surely, Galbraith is tripped up by his inconsistency concerning the growth motive. It is true that at the present time the large corporations have shown little interest in a technological revolution that could provide satisfactory housing cheaply enough for the present urban poor, but I would argue that this is not only for the obvious reason that the prospect lacks profitability, but because, in turn, unprofitability would react on growth. . . . We can, therefore, predict that merely providing a technical outlet will not do the trick. On the other hand, we can easily agree that providing both cash and technical outlet would be likely to succeed. The acid test of Galbraith's hypothesis would be the outcome in the event that cash was provided without any special steps on the technical front.[34]

(c) The position of the capitalist

We (unlike Galbraith) have already suggested that the locus of decision-making in the modern corporation is with the managers, not the technostructure. It is now necessary to go further and advance reasons why, despite the celebrated managerial revolution and the alleged separation of ownership from control, it is unlikely that the interests of the managers will be very much at odds with those of the capitalists.

To begin with, symbiosis rather than dichotomy often obtains between managers and shareholders. After all, many managers enjoy profit-sharing schemes or hold stock-options (despite Galbraith's insistence that 'stock holdings by management are small and often non-existent'[35]); and most, being well-off, probably are substantial shareholders in their own right (either in their own or in other corporations). This being the case, they are likely to represent the interests of the whole body of shareholders in guiding company policy. Nor should we forget that many technocrats themselves hold share-portfolios of one kind or another.

Moreover, Galbraith argues that dividends cannot be neglected if the technostructure is to enjoy autonomy, and admits that 'a rate of earnings that allows, over and above investment needs, for a progressive rise in the dividend rate will also regularly be a goal of the technostructure'.[36] The shareholders are naturally unable to know if their corporation has deliberately gone past the point of long-run profit-maximisation in order to expand sales or to try out an amusing new invention, but they are likely as a group to become restive should the firm fail to attain at least a threshold level of profit. It would be incorrect too to say that they have no sanctions to apply. They can easily sell out if profits are not in line with alternative opportunities (thereby leaving the shares of the corporation undervalued and inviting aggression from the technostructure of another firm, seeking to use a take-over as a cheap means of expansion). And they can make their discontent known at the Annual General Meeting. This is hardly an exercise in illusion even in the modern corporate economy for two reasons. Firstly, huge blocs of shares are today owned by institutional investors who cannot afford to neglect returns: the balance sheet of an insurance company, for example, reflects the income received on its investment portfolio, and the technostructure of one corporation is hardly likely to favour the growth and security of another at the expense of profits and hence of its own growth and security. In this way institutional investors may come to exercise pressure on behalf of the body of shareholders as a whole. Then, secondly, it would be wrong to underestimate present-day concentration of holdings (even greater if we focus on voting shares): at the very time that Galbraith was completing *The New Industrial State*, the controlling interest in 150 out of the 500 largest American corporations rested in the hands of one very wealthy individual or the members of a single family.[37] The death of the traditional proprietor has clearly been announced prematurely. Moreover, dispersion of share-ownership need not mean dispersion of power: quite small blocs of shares can be adequate for a successful shareholders' revolt (since not all shareholders choose to get involved) and a determined clique can if necessary form a coalition in order to impose its will. The fact is that changes in management do occur, and that in many companies managers truly are no better than their last balance sheet. The hypothesis of separation of ownership from control must thus be treated with the utmost caution. While it undeniably holds for the day-to-day operations of the corporation, it is likely that in the last analysis power results from ownership. And owners are likely to place a high valuation on the rate of return.

Consider now another point concerning the position of the capitalist, namely the possible conflict between distribution of profits and their reinvestment. Understandably, earning profits is not enough to ensure growth. The profits must also be ploughed back – i.e. the shareholder must be convinced of the benefit of putting future satisfactions ahead of present pleasures. Fortunately, even a policy of reinvestment and low dividends will favour the owner (and not simply the technocrat). After all, growth and additional profits are likely to lead to higher equity values, making shares that much more secure and lucrative as savings instruments. And realisation as well as accrual benefits the capitalist, notably in countries where dividends are subject to progressive income tax (often supplemented by an investment income surcharge) while capital gains tax on disposal of assets is payable at a flat rate. In such a situation, a wealthy shareholder would desire maximum long-term share-price appreciation rather than maximum annual dividends, and might feel distinctly friendly to a policy of sacrificing short-run dividends for the sake of long-run growth in the underlying assets and profitability of the corporation in oligopolistic markets where growth is essential for survival. He would not, however, back just any dash for growth, and would oppose unnecessary expansion which reduced the market value of his shares. In such a case the corporate bureaucrats might benefit but the owners would not, and the owners are not likely to conceal their disapproval.

Again, the assertion that dependence on the capital market has been minimised does not imply that such dependence has been eliminated. Not all funds are internally generated, and much needs to be raised via bond and share issues, or through borrowing from financial intermediaries – and here too profit plays a role. Clearly, prospective shareholders, acting on the recommendations of well-informed investment analysts, will not be bamboozled by the fact that the corporation always makes a profit (in a buoyant economy, few reasonably efficient firms consistently make actual losses and those which do are most likely to be nationalised enterprises with access to governmental subsidy), and will be reluctant to buy into an undertaking with an infra-competitive rate of return. And as for lenders, profits are bound to loom large in their considerations since they are concerned with the ability of the corporation to repay its debt. A low rate of profit, in short, may reduce the credit-rating and thus the capacity of the corporation to raise outside funds at the very time when its own internal supply of finance is inadequate. This will be particularly significant in countries where taxation discriminates against retained earnings and managers cannot depend on plough-ing back but must actively compete for savings: a perfect capital market may force managers to maximise profits so as to maximise the bait to investors and thus the inflow of new capital (while simultaneously minimising humiliating criticism in the press). It is, of course, easier to be lazy where taxation favours reinvestment in the progenitor-corporation (even should rates of return be higher elsewhere in the economy). Galbraith does not, however, propose measures such as penal taxation of retained earnings as a technique for encouraging the optimal allocation of resources and hence more rapid growth in the economy as a whole (in contrast to that of one particularly well-endowed. corporation). Here as elsewhere, Galbraith may justly be criticised for neglecting the problem of economic waste and for treating inefficiency as incidental.

Finally, there is not, statistically speaking, a dramatic difference in profit-rates as between owner-operated and bureaucratically run corporations, which suggests a certain similarity of motivation. Statistics on rates of profit must naturally be approached with some caution and with an eye to the relevant time-horizon. A firm, may, for example, seek to maximise sales in the short-run regardless of the rate of return on investment as part of a long-run competitive strategy to establish a powerful market position and thus *ultimately* to maximise profits; and alternative strategies may also be hy-pothesised. Nonetheless, it is not inherently implausible that both types of corporation do in fact react in the same way, and the reason is competition. For one thing, potential new entrants can often force existing firms to be efficient and profit-conscious: small firms can bid ground away from a sluggish giant (as General Motors did from Ford in the 1930s) by exploiting new ideas the large firm may have ignored. Then, too, there is the problem of pressure from existing rivals. Galbraith underestimates such challenge because he over-estimates complementarity of interest and believes, as we shall see, that even competitors are secure from one another.

In conclusion, it is perhaps worthwhile recapitulating our generally sceptical attitude to Galbraith's account of the techno-structure and its goals. We have argued that power in the modern corporation has most likely not devolved from managers to specialists, and that Galbraith has furthermore exaggerated the disappearance of proprietary controls over the running of the firm and also the extent to which maximum sales and maximum profits are substitutes rather than complements. It must be emphasised, however, that our scepticism extends only to Galbraith's specific hypotheses, and not to his general approach. Galbraith focuses his attention on men rather than things, on social interaction rather than resource allocation, and he develops a behaviouristic and institutionalist model which seeks in the first instance to explain precisely those variables which are traditionally concealed under the blanket assumption of *ceteris paribus*. Galbraith's broad and sociologically informed methodological orientation with respect to economics is quite distinct from the specific assertions which he chooses to make, and it is very easy indeed to be an enthusiastic admirer of the former while remaining somewhat sceptical with respect to the latter.

3 The Technological Imperative

Galbraith believes that the giant mature corporation differs both quantitatively and qualitatively from the small entrepreneurial firm of the elementary economics textbook, and in this chapter we will examine the nature of that difference. In Section I we will examine the case for size; in Section II the techniques of corporate planning that are utilised by the technostructure in pursuit of its goals; and in Section III the position of the small perfect competitor in our contemporary dual economy. In Section IV we will offer a critique of Galbraith's views on the technological imperative.

I THE CASE FOR SIZE

Large means few, but Galbraith is hostile neither to size nor to concentration since he identifies the huge firm operating in highly oligopolised markets as an important source of economic progress. Such progress takes the form, firstly, of a high propensity to innovate, and, secondly, of a high propensity to bear risk.

Consider first the case of research and development. The large firm has the resources to finance substantial laboratories and to staff them with well-qualified scientists and engineers, while the small firm simply cannot afford such expenditures, since they are a fixed cost only supportable at a large scale of output. Similarly, since not all projects in the end pay off, research must be done on a scale sufficiently large that successes and failures at least cancel out.

Moreover, it is a characteristic of oligopolistic structures (markets where there are a small number of large competitors) that firms are reluctant to alter their own prices because of uncertainty as to how their rivals will react and prefer to compete via non-price techniques, which of course include technological advance and product development, alongside intensive advertising.

Finally, because in an oligopolistic situation each product has an image of its own, even if rivals imitate an innovation the higher profits that it generates will still continue to accrue over time. In more perfectly competitive markets, on the other hand, once competitors copy the development (which seldom is fully protected by law), then the profits of all firms in the industry (including those of the initial innovator) return to the minimum level necessary to retain existing firms in the industry without attracting new entrants. Clearly, lack of product-differentiation is a disincentive to make the innovation in the first place: there is no reason to undergo costs if there is to be no special reward to compensate for them.

In fact, as well as in theory, the large firm is the source of technological advance: in 1967, for example, firms with fewer than 1000 employees accounted for only 4 per cent of research and development expenditure in the American economy, while the 274 firms with 10,000 or more employees accounted for 84 per cent.[1] The cotton textiles and shoe industries in the United States are not technologically progressive, and in agriculture almost all research is done not by the farmer but by the government or the large corporations which sell to the farmer. The lone inventor or small firm in the 'market system' (i.e. that sector of the economy where conditions most closely approach those of the perfectly competitive model) could not have got astronauts into space or sent men to the moon: 'No important technical development of recent times – atomic energy and its applications, modern air transport, modern electronic development, computer development, major agricultural innovation – is the product of the individual inventor in the market system. Individuals still have ideas. But – with rare exceptions – only organizations can bring ideas into use.'[2]

The large firm is outstandingly successful in both invention and innovation, and this in turn means improvement in product and reduction in cost. Such a clear benefit to the consumer must be weighed against the well-known market power that large size also implies, and it must be borne in mind that losses do have their offsets: 'A slight continuing loss of efficiency, as compared with ideal performance, from the possession of market power is regularly offset and more than offset by large gains from technical development. . . . In concentrating on the inefficiency of the steam engine – specifically the fact that it is not being worked at ideal capacity – [economists] have failed to notice that the owner was designing a gas turbine.'[3]

In reality, imperfect competition and technological progress are closely associated, and the latter justifies the existence of the former: the corporation has the power to set prices above the competitive norm in order to increase its revenues (while simultaneously reducing the volume of goods sold to the final consumer), but it also has the means and incentive to improve its technology and shift its whole supply function outwards. The resultant of these two forces cannot, of course, be predicted; but Galbraith believes it is likely to be lower prices and greater quantity sold than would have been the case even under competitive conditions. Perfect competition need not be the symbol of all that is good and in the public interest. In practice, the showpieces of American industry are the large corporations: 'The foreign visitor, brought to the United States to study American production methods and associated marvels, visits the same firms as do attorneys of the Department of Justice in their search for monopoly.'[4]

Let us consider now Galbraith's second argument in support of the huge firm, namely its high propensity to bear risk. The problem here is that a great deal of capital (both fixed and working) is required by the large corporation, and most of it is sector-specific. This means a very heavy initial commitment of funds, and also that the failure to sell the product is an expensive proposition: plant is inflexible and cannot be converted to an alternative use without much difficulty and after a considerable time-lag. Moreover, the corporation is vulnerable for another reason: the long gestation period between the time a project is planned and the time the final product is actually put on the market. Here too there is a heavy financial commitment to non-transferable plant for a lengthy period, and thus a high cost well before returns on the investment begin to be realised (coupled with the possibility of failure to realise such gains at all).

The costly commitment of advanced technology and capital substantially in advance of marketing the final product imposes considerable uncertainty on the producer, and this the modern corporation copes with by 'planning'. The modern corporation lives in the future; it attempts to forecast the future needs and desires of the buyer, often by years; and it seeks also to anticipate future supply conditions of its inputs. Moreover, the modern corporation not only attempts to predict the future business environment but aims also to control it, in order to emancipate itself from the vagaries of the market mechanism. For the large capital-intensive firm, in other words, there already exists a privately planned economy, and free enterprise itself has already suppressed the market in the interests of prediction: it is simply too risky to throw an increased quantity of computers or supersonic aircraft on to the market and then wait for consumer demand to determine price charged and quantity sold. The very exploitation of advanced technology (whether in a capitalist or a socialist economy) presupposes considerable control by the producer over conditions of sale:

> The modern large corporation and the modern apparatus of socialist planning are variant accommodations to the same need. It is open to every free-born man to dislike this accommodation. But he must direct his attack to the cause. He must not ask that jet aircraft, nuclear power plants or even the modern automobile in its modern volume be produced by firms that are subject to unfixed prices and unmanaged demand. He must ask instead that they not be produced.[5]

The larger the size of the firm, the greater is its ability to influence its environment. Size means strength, and a firm wishing to 'plan' may thus deliberately grow so large as to be incurring diminishing returns to scale in terms of output per unit of input:

> For any given level and use of technology there is, no doubt, a technically optimum size of firm – the size which most economically sustains the requisite specialists, the counterpart organization and the associated capital investment. But the need to control environment – to exclude untoward events – encourages much greater size. The larger the firm, the larger it will be in its industry. The greater, accordingly, will be its influence in setting prices and costs. And the greater, in general, will be its influence on consumers, the community and the state – the greater, in short, will be its ability to influence, i.e., plan, its environment.[6]

Here size is desired not chiefly to reap technological economies of large scale or even to increase profits, but rather because size is essential for planning. Moreover, 'for this planning – control of supply, control of demand, provision of capital, minimization of risk – there is no clear upper limit to the desirable size'[7]. Size is a precondition for domination, and many a small firm is bound to envy General Motors, which in 1968 had gross revenues 'more than a hundred times the revenue of the state of Nevada, more than three times the total revenue of the state of New York and about one eighth of the total receipts of the federal government'.[8] General Motors clearly has clout and demonstrates yet again that bigger is better when the objective is control.

II CORPORATE PLANNING

The techniques that the large firm uses in order to 'plan' its markets fall neatly into six groups, each representing its relationship with a different part of the economy.

First, the corporation attempts to ensure consumer response to the product such that a targeted quantity at a targeted price can be sold. This we shall consider in Chapter 5.

Second, the corporation seeks to secure financial aid and guaranteed markets from the State. This we shall consider in Chapter 6.

Third, the corporation establishes a matrix of inter-firm contracts. The outputs (and prices) of one firm are typically the inputs (and costs) of another, and firms can hence guarantee each other both secure supplies of materials and components and secure markets at predictable prices. The web of interlocking contracts ensures stability to its participants, permits them to plan ahead, and allows them to extend the safety-net of certainty to still more firms (since an enterprise with one agreement is in a strong position to conclude other agreements). The network also ensures some consistency and coordination of production plans (an advantage which the free market does not offer, partly due to the time-lag between a rise in prices and the resultant rise in quantity supplied).

Such agreements are concluded amicably: the business-world of today shows substantially less aggression than when capitalist entrepreneurs fought over a given mass of profit, and the reason is that the prices and quantities agreed upon are set not with a view to competition but with the security and growth of both parties to the contract in mind. Nowadays, 'the prices that serve the growth of one firm will, generally speaking, serve the growth of others. One firm, accordingly, can set prices knowing that others will find them broadly acceptable.'[9] One firm could not, of course, so amicably set prices that maximised its own profit or market share at the expense of its neighbour, but firms in the new industrial state recognise their interdependence and their common protective and affirmative purposes. This leads to a sensation of cooperation and cordiality, of one hand washing the other, that contrasts sharply with the nastiness that prevailed in the bad old days when firms maximised profits rather than growth.

Fourth, there is integration. In the interests of availability and predictability, the corporation may choose to integrate backwards (say, by taking over oil-wells and mines), forwards (say, by securing a chain of retailing outlets), or horizontally (by taking over a competitor). In all cases, the primary objective is not profits but the attainment of organisational goals.

Integration may occur on an international scale. The large firm may, for example, integrate backwards into supplies of raw materials found not at home but abroad. Such integration into primary production is unlikely to indicate that a profit-motivated enterprise is trying to obtain a base from which to merchandise its surplus output in the Third World. Developing countries are not important outlets for the products of metropolitan areas, and if a mature corporation expands there the objective is more likely to be materials than markets. Its aim is almost certainly merely to guarantee its own supplies by making price and quantity of inputs decisions internal to the firm.

Again, the mature corporation may go multinational by producing and marketing abroad the same product as it produces and markets at home. By expanding in this way, the corporation seeks to neutralise the uncertainties associated with international trade in the same spirit as older policy-instruments (tariffs, export levies, devaluation, quotas, embargoes) sought to insulate the firm and protect it against the old-style vicissitudes of competition. The multinational firm is able to influence consumer, State and other economic actors abroad in the same way as it does at home, and thus replaces competition by planning on a world-wide scale. Such planning need not be in the public interest, but in discussing this aspect of a phenomenon which some commentators to the left of Galbraith consider 'economic imperialism' it is vital to remember that the nationality of the firm in Galbraith's view is without importance: the foreign firm, economically speaking, is no more a threat than the domestic corporation (and, of course, no less). The only major additional disadvantage from the host country's point of view is this: the multinational corporation, precisely because it is multinational and operates in a number of countries simultaneously, is able in practice to establish its own common markets independent of the much-publicised attempts of elected governments to do so.

Should the corporation not wish to go multinational, it may (once it has saturated its domestic market for a particular commodity) choose to diversify and become a conglomerate. Galbraith (who admittedly came late to the question of the conglomerate and has not had a great deal to say about it) believes that there is little technological justification for a corporation whose activities are unrelated and whose products are an illogical mix (so illogical that they may not be complementary or even depend on similar technical expertise and marketing skills). Expansion via diversification is not without its attractions, however. For one thing, while the conglomerate is naturally not able to control prices and quantities in particular markets where its share is small, it is likely to have influence with government by virtue of its giant aggregate size. And again, growth via diversification into a number of markets also represents security against risk, since losses in one area will hopefully be counterbalanced by gains in another; and this satisfies the protective as well as the affirmative purpose of the firm.

Fifth, the corporation attempts through retained earnings to insulate itself from the hazards of the capital market. Reinvestment of internally generated (but not distributed) funds ensures that the expansion of the firm and its technostructure will not be retarded by a credit squeeze or a sudden rise in the cost of borrowing. Moreover, a substantial pool of earnings to be ploughed back as investment means that the corporation, having secure internal sources of finance, will not need to sacrifice the autonomy of its technostructure to bankers and other outside lenders (who ask embarrassing questions, impose awkward conditions, are intolerant of the occasional failure even where risky innovation is essential for job-satisfaction, and might want to send in a team of outside management consultants).

More generally, 'the security that is associated with an ample flow of funds from internal sources will favor the firm so blessed when it goes into the capital markets for additional supplies'.[10] And outside finance is not difficult in any case to attract: a growing and wealthy economy tends to develop a pool of surplus savings (Galbraith is true to the spirit of Keynes in this respect[11]) and the resultant competition among lenders for borrowers permits the technostructure to select the most attractive terms with the minimum risk of interference. Besides that, no financier can possibly understand the needs of the firm as well as the technostructure, and hence would-be creditors are likely to bow to its superior (collective) intelligence. In summary, even if finance from outside the firm is needed, this does not mean that such finance will necessarily involve intervention from uninformed strangers.

Sixth, the corporation attempts to neutralise disruption on the part of the labour force (the input least under corporate control with respect both to price and to availability). Two techniques are used to deal with this troublesome and unreliable factor, namely displacement and pacification.

The first expedient, displacement, refers to mechanisation, i.e. the substitution of capital for labour: the corporation quite simply deals with uncertainty associated with the price of labour (the problem, say, of trade unions) and its availability (since the supply of skilled labour is exogenous to the firm and provided by the State-controlled education industries) via automation. The decision to substitute machines for men is not based on comparison of costs (as many orthodox economists assert) but on the need for reliability and predictability. The fact is that, in the world of the large corporation, most savings are internally generated (whereas the firm cannot supply labour to itself); the price of capital is relatively stable because of inter-firm contracts and constant once the plant has been purchased; and machines, once installed, 'do not go on strike'.[12] Clearly, innovation does not only take place in the market for new consumer goods; it also serves the protective purpose of the technostructure by enabling it to replace a factor not under its control by one that is.

The second expedient is pacification: here the corporation meets the workers' demands for higher pay by conceding them. Sometimes there are productivity schemes linked to the rise in wages, but where there are not dividends may be cut or prices charged to the final consumer raised. Galbraith argues that, since the modern corporation is not a profit-maximiser, it could already have raised these prices, had it wished to do so: 'A firm that advances its prices after a wage increase could have done so before. At the previous lower costs and the higher prices it would have made more money.'[13] Yet it chose not to raise its prices on its own account. Such hesitation may be explained in terms of fear lest the corporation attract the attention of the unions (no longer a danger once the workers have attacked first) or the opprobrium of the public (but adverse publicity will not result once a rise in prices can be explained away as a reaction to a previous rise in wages). Again, the firm may have hesitated to raise its prices independently lest it upset the truce on price-competition in oligopolistic conditions: it could have lost its customers to its handful of equally powerful rivals had it raised its prices while they kept theirs constant (just as if it reduced its prices and was followed by its rivals, the net result would be that each had beggared his neighbour and gained nothing in return). Once the unions have attacked, however, then oligopolists can take the wage-rise as signal for and measure of a parallel rise in prices: because of industry-wide collective bargaining, wages typically rise simultaneously for all firms in the industry and by approximately the same amount.

Higher prices of the product may discourage sales and retard the rate of growth of the corporation, certainly a blow to a technostructure pursuing a policy of sales-expansion out of unrealised profits. However, the alternative to raising prices might have been not raising wages; and a prolonged and nasty strike might be even more disruptive of planned growth, as well as reducing future worker-identification with the firm and tarnishing the corporate image (prestige being an important fringe benefit for the organisation man). In any case, the elasticity of demand may be on the side of the firm: a higher price of the good, if accompanied by a less-than-proportional fall in quantity demanded, may increase the pool of profits available for future investment and thus accelerate the ultimate expansion of the firm.

The twin techniques of displacement and pacification which the mature corporation employs to ensure the reliability and predictability of its labour force help to explain the gradual disappearance of class conflict and the class struggle. This is not to deny that it ever existed. On the contrary, historically speaking, the labour-market is 'the oldest arena of conflict in capitalism'. Here the choice facing the worker is 'whether the boss will be boss or not — whether he will be able to exercise authority over wages and working conditions and enjoy unimpaired powers of command, or whether he will share this authority. Economic life poses few more obscenely naked problems of prestige and of power and also of income.'[14] In the modern corporation, this conflict seems finally resolved.

For one thing, a rising percentage of the corporate labour-force is brainy rather than brawny. Such men enjoy good pay, their work is interesting and not physically taxing, and they feel closer to the technostructure than to the union. Increasingly, 'distinctions between those who make decisions and those who carry them out, and between employer and employee, are obscured by the technicians, scientists, market analysts, computer programmers, industrial stylists and other specialists who do, or are, both. A continuum thus exists between the centre of the technostructure and the more routine white-collar workers on the fringe.'[15] In this way *embourgeoisement* too enhances the security of the specialists.

Moreover, even the manual labourers 'become an extension of the technostructure and evidently so see themselves'.[16] After all, the goals of the one group are the goals of the other, namely job-satisfaction, security (which to the worker means steady employment and no redundancies) and growth (which to the worker means more voluntary overtime, more promotions, more jobs for the boys). Once loyalty to the firm and identification with its objectives come to coexist with the cash nexus, there is a greater likelihood that harmony will replace militancy and a diminished probability that the worker will go on strike.

Again, there is less scope for confrontation in collective bargaining. The willingness of the technostructure to raise prices or cut dividends rather than to resist demands for a wage rise builds a cost-push inflationary bias into the system and represents the emergence of a great coalition against the consumer and the shareholder, but it also suggests that disputes will be settled peacefully, since there is little case for class-conflict between two groups of paid employees. As a result, nowadays a sensation of 'shared responsibility and shared gain'[17] has replaced any previous sense of exploitation, and this is a source both of tranquillity and of progress: 'If development is to depend on popular participation, then there must be a system of popular rewards. There can be no effective advance if the masses of the people do not participate; man is not so constituted that he will bend his best energies for the enrichment of someone else. As literacy is economically efficient, so is social justice.'[18]

Furthermore, the unions, although their membership is now, in the United States, in decline, also contribute to the eradication of class conflict. They act as a channel of communications between production workers and management, and thus help to prevent potential feelings of alienation and powerlessness. The unions also assist in the orderly introduction of new technology (especially ticklish where machines replace men), are essential to the process of planning in oligopolistic conditions (by ensuring that no firm will have higher or lower prices because of higher or lower wages) and join their voice to management in requesting government contracts (say, by pointing out that otherwise there will be redundancies among their members) and in opposing State intervention in the wage-bargain.

Finally, class conflict is nowadays in decline for the simple reason that wealth itself is becoming 'less a source of prestige'[19] relative to, say, intellectual or political achievement. In the late nineteenth century a rich capitalist like John D. Rockefeller stood out because of his riches. In our time, however, 'no man of wealth enjoys comparable distinction. Nor is esteem associated with individuals; by the nature of the technostructure they are submerged in the group. Esteem is associated with corporations.'[20]

III THE MARKET SYSTEM

Not all firms in the new industrial state are able to dominate their markets. In reality, Western economies (analogous to those of under-developed countries) are dual economies, where the corporate 'planning system' (with its power willy nilly to influence its environment) coexists side by side with the traditional 'market system' (a mass of small, competitive firms, passive with respect to price charged and quantity sold, subordinate to economic forces they cannot control). The systems are approximately equal in size in so far as each supplies about half the goods and services generated in the domestic private sector.[21]

In the market system, the consumer is still basically sovereign and the small-scale firm is still basically a price-taker: advertising is prohibitively expensive and products tend in any case to be undifferentiated and homogeneous. In the market system, moreover, 'market incentives obviously make people work hard'[22]; and this applies as well to the entrepreneur (since maximum profits are essential if the firm is to survive). Thus, the market system conforms more or less to the orthodox textbook picture of market capitalism, and the neoclassical model describes about half the economy with some success. Even this is subject to some modification, however, due to factors such as local monopoly (say, where there is business enough for only one restaurant in a locality and the presence of two would cause both entrepreneurs to starve, albeit a diminished threat in the era of the motor-car) or product differentiation (as where each of a number of self-employed plumbers has a different personality or degree of skill). In such cases the firm acquires some measure of control over prices and production. Normally, however, it demonstrates the passivity characteristic of the perfect competitor.

Competitive small-scale production is likely to be found where the task cannot easily be standardised, where production is geographically dispersed (although the large firm can break into such a market through franchising schemes), where there is a demand for a local personal service, where the artistic component in production is substantial (artists are not easily absorbed into organisations and when they are tend to lose their greatest powers of creativity), where there are legal restrictions on the growth of the firm, professional ethics limiting its size, or a ceiling on expansion imposed by a professional body such as the American Medical Association. Some examples of enterprises in the American market system are the small farmer, shopkeeper, textile manufacturer, and most of the service trades (plumbers, doctors, photographers, shoe repairmen). Since an affluent society is likely to favour many of these activities, there is no reason to expect the market system to decline still further.

The two systems are approximately equal in size. They are not, however, approximately equal in power. The large firm has capital, organisation and advanced technology on its side, and is able to turn the domestic terms of trade in its favour: it can, after all, exploit and bully the weaker market system, since it has the power to influence the prices at which it buys from and sells to the small firm, and thus the power to impose its goals on non-corporate producers. In a dual economy in which large and active corporations (run by and for specialist technocrats) coexist with small and passive firms (run by owner-entrepreneurs and subject to the profit motive), tremendous inequality of resources obtains. For example:

> The two largest industrial corporations, General Motors and Exxon, have combined revenues far exceeding those of California and New York. . . . The 333 industrial corporations with assets of more than $500 million had a full 70 per cent of all assets employed in manufacturing. . . . An assembly of the heads of the firms doing half of all the business in the United States would,

except in appearance, be unimpressive in a university auditorium and nearly invisible in the stadium.[23]

And because this concentration of wealth so clearly represents a concentration of power, it is more probable that the large corporation (not the State) is a threat to the individual freedom of the small firm and the cause of the systemic inequality in returns and development as between the two systems that arises from differential power.

Systemic inequality affects workers as well as firms. In the market system there is no cost-push inflation since the small entrepreneur is a passive price-taker, while in the planning system large corporations tend to concede union demands without a struggle, and this leads to substantial differences in pay within the economy. The fact is that the small entrepreneur cannot afford to pay high wages, and can only survive through the exploitation not only of his workers but also of himself and his family (witness low pay and long hours on the farm). Such self-exploitation enjoys widespread social approval, but approval is apparently inadequate to content the workers. They, 'the exploited',[24] are more likely to move out of the market system (where pay is low) into the planning system (where pay is high). Those who remain behind are likely to be those who, because of race, lack of education and skill, inconvenient geographical location or inertia, are unable to participate in this equalising process, and they are understandably likely to be resentful: a major contemporary social problem is the low-paid, unskilled black youth in a depressed slum area, whose factor mobility approaches zero.

Clearly, the small-scale, competitive market system need not be synonymous with all that is good in the American way of life. It is in the market system that much of the greatest misery and inequality is nowadays to be found. In the market system, moreover, there is inadequate innovation, since there is little capital to cover research and development costs, the purchase of expensive machinery, and the long gestation period before a new product is marketed. More generally, some of the worst cases of mismanagement in American economic history have been the fault of that great folk-hero, the owner-entrepreneur. Consider in this context the case of Henry Ford: 'In the thirties and early forties the elder Henry Ford used his power as the sole owner of the Ford Motor Company to remain in command. It is now freely acknowledged that the company suffered severely as a result. Following his death the management was professionalised and much improved.'[25] Ford's resistance to innovation and continued insistence on the Model T meant obsolescence of product and loss of sales to competitors. He did not fully understand balance sheets and cost accounts; paid no attention to marketing, advertising and consumer preferences; had no knowledge of physics and chemistry, and little of engineering (he either couldn't or wouldn't read blueprints); sponsored little research and development because he distrusted university-educated men; purged executives who were progressive and go-ahead in their business policies. Even his world-famous economic philosophy had to be ghost-written for him by Samuel Crowther, who authored every word of Ford's three books.[26] Hero worship of the owner-entrepreneur can evidently be misplaced; and there is much to be said in favour of the organisation man.

IV EVALUATION

In this section we will attempt to evaluate Galbraith's views on the technological imperative:

(a) The case for size

In considering Galbraith's assertion that most significant technological innovation originates in the large corporations of the planning system, it is valuable to look at the evidence. Here, Myron Sharpe has pointed out, first, that 'most of the new products introduced in the postwar period originated from individual inventions or from research conducted by small and medium-sized firms' (products such as, for example, electric refrigerators, dishwashers and dryers, safety razor blades, jet engines); and, second, that 'Galbraith doesn't distinguish between the sources of invention and their application. Many inventions originated with individuals or small firms but could be produced and marketed successfully only by giant corporations because of capital and time requirements. . . . Typically a small firm pioneers development and production, and after the product has proven its value, a large firm takes over, buying out or squeezing out the small one.'[27]

This suggests that, technologically speaking, the small firm is not merely a survival from a previous stage of economic evolution and that its track-record in technical progress might not really be inferior to that of the giant oligopolist. Besides, even if the large corporation is efficient, it need not be beneficient: Galbraith does not explain how the gains from higher productivity via improvement in production-processes (in contrast to the development of new consumables, to which he confines most of his discussion of technological advance) are passed on to the consumer, at least in an oligopolistic market-structure where rigid prices are the rule. In such circumstances, big need not be beautiful.

Galbraith's views on the dynamic and progressive nature of large organisations conflict with other analyses of bureaucratised structures which tend to bring out their conservatism, fear of upset and change, lethargy, rigidity, and distrust of exceptional ability which cannot easily be regimented into planned programmes. Indeed, if the giant corporations of the planning system are in fact earning below-average profits, the real reason might simply be bureaucratic inertia (coupled with waste of resources due to internally generated information-costs and communication-failures). In reality (and despite Galbraith's assertion that the large corporation can plan and control its markets), many traditional industries have been experiencing slower growth than some newer ones because of a shift in consumer preferences. Faced with this challenge, some low-performance corporations have nonetheless refused to diversify, and this extraordinary inertia is likely to reflect vested interest as much as the cost of building new plant and penetrating new markets.

By way of contrast, small firms often retain the flexibility and the pioneering spirit which many large firms have lost. This is probably especially true in the burgeoning service industries, as Maurice Zinkin has pointed out for the United Kingdom:

> In the service industries it is obvious that the talent which most effectively changes the consumer's tastes and best responds to the consumer's desires, lies in the small firm rather than the big. Mary Quant has had more effect on fashion than all the department stores put together. It was the relatively small travel agencies, not the great airlines, which invented the package holiday. The idea of high quality food on a limited menu was invented by new firms like Angus Steak Houses and Golden Egg, not the old-established J. Lyons. It was the owner-driver with a lorry or two, rather than the large haulage firms, who originally

took the traffic away from the railways. Even the major supermarket companies are largely new; many of the old multiple retailers were slow to see the possibilities of this new form of retailing.[28]

In short, the small firm does indulge in both process and product innovation, and the large firm remains vulnerable to encroachment from dynamic new competitors precisely because of its own slowness to react. In reality, both the small firm and the spur of competition have a greater role to play in the process of technical improvement than Galbraith is prepared to admit.

As to Galbraith's second argument in defence of size – namely that much of capital is inflexible and sector-specific – it is worth noting that this assertion too may be exaggerated. Plant installed to produce computers may be sector-specific to the computer industry but can nonetheless be modified to produce many types of computer. Plant installed to produce cars could be used to produce tractors or milk-floats. Such flexibility suggests that the firm is less at the mercy of unforeseen events than Galbraith would appear to believe. It is even possible he has fallen victim to the special pleading of the technostructure itself. Rather than being progressive and energetic titans, they may turn out to be frightened and grey little men who fear they have non-transferable skills when in fact they have just got into a rut.

(b) Corporate planning

With respect to Galbraith's assertion that the corporate sector of a modern capitalist country represents a 'planned economy', it will by now have become evident that this result owes much to what the *Daily Telegraph* once characterised as Galbraith's 'slight of mouth'. He uses the term 'planning' in a peculiar sense, to refer to the attempt of the technostructure of the large corporation both to forecast the future and to shape it. On both accounts, however, his analysis is incomplete.

Firstly, the model is incomplete in so far as it involves forecasts of the future for the simple reason that Galbraith does not explain how the microeconomic plans of individual firms become coordinated into a coherent national macroeconomic plan. If the price-mechanism ceases to be a regulator, then some other regulator must be found, and it is this alternative regulator which is conspicuously absent in Galbraith's analysis. James Meade has explained the problem as follows:

> Professor Galbraith asserts that each modern corporation plans ahead the quantities of the various products which it will produce and the prices at which it will sell them; he assumes . . . that as a general rule each corporation through its advertising and other sales' activities can so mould consumers' demands that these planned quantities are actually sold at these planned prices. But he never explains why and by what mechanism these individual plans can be expected to build up into a coherent whole. What happens, for example, if all the steel-using industries plan outputs of products made from steel which require more (or less) steel than the planned outputs of the steel-making industry? Or what happens if the sum of all the individual plans of all the corporations leads to a demand for labour which is much greater (or less) than the available supply? . . . In short, if all individual plans are to be simultaneously fulfilled they must in the first instance be consistent. But Professor Galbraith never considers this problem. It is a strange insight in a modern professional economist—to overlook the problem of general, as contrasted with particular, equilibrium.[29]

It is certainly a valid criticism to say that Galbraith moves from arguing that the firm plans to insisting that the economy is planned without explaining why coherence and harmony should result when all individual plans are aggregated. In Galbraith's defence, however, it is worthwhile noting the multitude of techniques at the disposal of the firm (such as long-term inter-firm contracts or forward and backward integration) which do raise the degree of coordination in the economy, and also that to Galbraith planning is not merely forecasting but action (and each firm is alleged to be capable of making realistic assumptions about its ability to shape future markets). Moreover, in *Economics and the Public Purpose* (possibly in response to Meade's criticisms of his earlier work), Galbraith ultimately does call for some form of national economic planning in order to ensure that performance in related parts of the economy really does match. We shall be considering his outline proposals for national economic planning in Chapter 6.

Secondly, the model is incomplete in so far as Galbraith overstates the extent to which the large corporation is the master of the environment in which it operates. Expensive failures of planning are mentioned,[30] but Galbraith seems to regard them as mere exceptions which prove the rule. Basically, as Scott Gordon puts it, the corporation in the Galbraithian world 'controls completely all the important elements of its environment. It has no need to accommodate itself to any exogenous circumstances; it is able to mold these to suit itself. Such a corporation would be like no organism, biological or social, that ever was, for it would encounter no constraints upon what it wishes (or is impelled) to do, which is to grow. Theoretically, we should observe all major industrial firms growing infinitely large, each of them – moreover, instantaneously.'[31]

In particular, one of the major difficulties facing one technostructure in the attainment of its goals is the existence of another technostructure which confronts it and with which it might well have to enter into conflict. Galbraith minimises this danger by arguing that corporations no longer compete for relative shares in a given market but all plan and grow together by means of a network of interlocking contracts. He even gives the instance of a firm losing customers to others which will merely improve its marketing and sales strategies so as to restore the equilibrium *status quo ante*.[32] He thus completely ignores the terms on which one technostructure contracts with another (the concept of 'countervailing power' might have been utilised here but is not) and also the threat of blood lust: the technostructures of two corporations are expected to regard each other as brothers rather than as enemies, and to substitute mutual expansion of sales for the primordial urge to bid away one another's profits. In fact, however, it may not make sense to argue as if the corporation is free from intense external competitive pressures and to postulate that one firm's sales strategy is no constraint on that of another. As Robert Fitch has pointed out, it is simply incorrect to assume that one firm can plan without taking its rivals into account: 'It is like saying that because two nations' armies follow their respective battle plans and the troops follow orders that the resulting war between them is "planned"'.[33] In reality, the corporation is free to plan ahead; but its targets may not be attained due to resistance from the consumer to its sales strategies or to competition from rivals with sales strategies of their own. Predictions are easily upset should 'planning' not prove fully successful.

Galbraith believes that the ability of the firm to influence its environment is intimately related to its size, and that the desire to plan successfully is an important reason for corporate growth. He further believes that there is no upper limit to the size of the firm since the larger it is, the greater its ability to minimise uncertainty and maximise power. Yet this too is a strange doctrine. To begin with, Galbraith appears to be confusing size with concentration (a confusion made worse by his failure to suggest actual measures of concentration and power) and focuses on firms rather than markets (whereas it does in fact matter a great deal whether there is one giant in an industry or twenty).[34] Moreover, he is once again underestimating the importance of waste: he argues that in order to dominate its market the large firm grows beyond the size necessary for optimal efficiency in production, but nonetheless omits to lament the misallocation of society's resources that results once the corporation has exhausted its economies of large scale.[35] Then, too, the techniques of growth are themselves highly relevant. If a firm integrates horizontally, it may (albeit purely in the interest of growth and security) be taking over competitors and converting itself into a monopoly, able (if it wished to do so) to raise prices and reduce quantity sold. If it integrates vertically, it may be eliminating such countervailing power of buyer to seller as might previously have existed (albeit simply because intra-firm transactions are more coordinated and secure than trade with outsiders, even where such trade is regulated by contract). But if it goes conglomerate, because it enjoys a smaller share of each individual market (and probably experiences greater internal decentralisation and democratisation in management), the corporation is actually forced to sacrifice power in order to secure growth and must compete more rather than less intensively as the price of its expansion. A strategy of growth via diversification rather than via domination of a single market may well tend to re-establish some form of workable competition as the central force in a capitalist economy; but Galbraith greatly under-estimates this tendency primarily because of his general propensity to treat the conglomerate as an exception, and corporations specialised and concentrated in a single industry as the rule.[36]

Finally, Galbraith exaggerates the extent to which the large corporation is the master of the environment in which it operates in his approach to the trade union and the process of collective bargaining. He believes, as we have seen, that (because the technostructure has the power to export inflation to other sectors of the economy and because decision-makers on a salary as well as workers on a wage can share in the gains from cost-push inflation that arise in the planning system), traditional class antagonisms have been replaced by a new climate of 'mellowness in collective bargaining. The employer who cannot get along with his union has become hopelessly *déclassé*. He is tactfully but firmly excluded from the list of after-luncheon speakers; he must himself listen to the modern hero, the man who has negotiated twenty contracts but never had a strike.'[37] In fact, however, it is unrealistic to dismiss the 'ceremonial insult'[38] which usually accompanies collective bargaining as sound without fury, or to extrapolate from the observed decline in trade union membership[39] to some presumed decline in trade union militancy. Hard bargaining between union and corporation accompany the introduction of new processes as well as claims for higher pay, and the strike is hardly an outdated weapon at such times.

More generally, while technostructure and workers share some goals (notably with respect to rising standards of living), there are others which they cannot share and which may breed resentment. The workers might, for example, be prepared to trade some growth of the corporation (particularly where they are not in a position to win promotion) for better sports and canteen facilities, more opportunities for day-release to acquire additional qualifications, more leisure enjoyed at place of work; or they may come to believe that they are economically exploited whenever the surplus value which they produce is siphoned off by the capitalist class. Again, the workers might (being, like the shareholders, left out in the cold when the firm comes to frame its rules and plan its future) resent the lack of opportunities for serious consultation and participation, and might – totally ignoring the fact that the middle-class technostructure does not differ significantly from the classical proletariat in terms of ownership of the means of production employed in the firm – challenge its autonomy to make decisions and command others to an extent which Galbraith (who typically regards power-sharing as deplorably detrimental to technological progress) would find inconvenient if not intolerable. Finally the workers might resent the fact that the bosses are better paid, enjoy higher status, consume more elegant status-symbols in enviably comfortable surroundings, and might despite upgrading experience jealousy of their whitest-collar colleagues.

In concluding our discussion of Galbraith's views on corporate planning, it is useful to re-state our general contention: Galbraith exaggerates, since a firm able to plan its own actions will not necessarily succeed in planning the reactions of others. Paul Samuelson was, in our view, perfectly right when he commented that Galbraith 'makes modern corporations into kings who rule unilaterally. They don't. They're constitutional monarchs; they try to shape the market, but they can't make the market react.'[40]

(c) The market system

It may, to begin with, be questioned whether it is helpful to set up a two-pole model at all rather than to speak in terms of a continuum of undertakings. Galbraith believes that 'little is lost and much is clarified'[41] if we work with such a model and situate on the one hand the powerful, on the other hand the powerless. An approach of this nature may be adequate if one is thinking purely in terms of ideal types. Galbraith, however, subtly moves from exposition to description and evidently is convinced that his model bears a strong resemblance to conditions in the real world: 'My assumption amounts to saying that an important part of the economy is like or approaches the organization of agriculture and that another important part approximates the organization of the steel industry. My conclusions are not altered in kind, although they will be quantitatively changed, by the distribution of industries in between.'[42] The question then becomes whether there is indeed an empirically ascertainable dividing-line between the two systems; for without such a dividing-line the two-pole model collapses into a spectrum and the concept of systemic inequality loses much of its attractive simplicity.

Even were there to exist two clearly defined systems, moreover, it would still be misleading to focus entirely on differences and to neglect the similarities that obtain between them. We have already suggested that the small firm is responsible for far more invention and innovation, and that the large corporation is far more market-orientated and profit-motivated, than is dreamt of in Galbraith's philosophy; and it is worthwhile adding to this list three further ways in which small and large tend to resemble one another. First, even small firms try to forecast and plan their futures (as, indeed, does the individual and the State), and for this reason it is foolish to argue as if the less powerful simply throw their output on to the market without any prior effort to discover what the consumer wants and at what price. Of course, it is easier for a small firm to make forecasts than it would be for that firm to try and shape its market; but then, as we have already argued, there are definite limits on the power of even the largest corporations successfully to mould the business environment in their desired image. Second, even small firms may come to depend on some sort of technostructure, for, as Frank McFadzean points out, 'as soon as a business ceases to be a one-man band . . . employees will know things that the owner does not',[43] and that technostructure will in turn use their knowledge and expertise selectively to further their own interests with respect to the normal organisational goals of job-satisfaction, security and growth. Third, even small firms may have power to dominate their market, for dominance is in truth a function not merely of absolute size but of the presence or absence of close substitutes, and many a shopper at the single store of an isolated mountain village may experience a sense of resentment from which the consumer with access to the multiple alternatives of the High Street (even if local branches of huge national chains) may prove mercifully free.

Looking to the future, the outlook for the small firm might be rosy rather than bleak for, in an even more affluent society, there might occur a boom in service industries with a high income elasticity but no particular economies of large scale (small firms in fields such as hairdressing salons, fashion boutiques, fringe theatres, after all, might actually be more sensitive than large ones to the changing demands of the post-industrial consumer). Galbraith, however, does not adopt this view of the future, and is not convinced that the anticipated expansion in the demand for final services (for services which are output, such as those of a restaurant, rather than for those which are input, such as those of the technostructure) will necessarily favour the independent producer and the competitive market: while it is true that the large firm is at present more important in manufacturing and finance than in service-trades, there is no reason to suppose that an extension of the chain and the franchise will not permit it in the future to penetrate deeply into enemy territory, assisted here by the fact that its small-scale rival is weak on mechanisation. Small size might mean flexibility, but large size means the power to dominate; and, while no one can say for sure whether history is on the side of the fox or of the dinosaur, Galbraith is evidently convinced that the future distribution of the GNP as between the two systems will not be radically different from that of today.

4 Countervailing Power

In a perfectly competitive economy, no individual producer can harm others without harming himself: if he cuts wages he will lose labour to other employers, if he raises prices he will lose his customers to his competitors, if he underpays his suppliers they will divert their goods to other firms. In such a situation the problem of power does not arise: no one buyer or seller has the ability to influence prices charged or quantities sold, or to impose his personal goals and decisions willy nilly on other individuals and groups. In such a situation, moreover, State intervention – save of the law and order variety – is widely held to be both unnecessary (free competition is itself adequate to ensure optimal and democratic allocation of resources) and undesirable (it constitutes a new locus of power in a world where power otherwise would be dispersed and impersonal).

Business concentration and the giant corporation mean, however, that we cannot avoid the problem of power in the modern economy, nor indeed the abuses that result from subordination; for whereas a perfect competitor dare not cut wages, raise prices or underpay suppliers, a monopolist or oligopolist is not subject to the same constraint. The socialist answer to this potential abuse of power is nationalisation, while liberals call for State action in the form of legislation to control mergers, regulate monopolies, combat restrictive practices. Galbraith, however, in his celebrated early book, *American Capitalism* (1952), chose to adopt a third position. His argument was that power exists, but that fortunately it exists in pairs; and that, although perfect competition may have disappeared from many markets, it has inevitably been replaced by an alternative self-regulating mechanism, so that State intervention in the functioning of markets remains unnecessary.

In this chapter we shall proceed as follows. In Section I we shall attempt to explain the theory of countervailing power; while in Section II we shall consider some criticisms of a theoretical insight which Galbraith himself subsequently in large measure abandoned.

I THE THEORY OF COUNTERVAILING POWER

Gailbraith notes as one of the paradoxes of American capitalism that, coincidental with the merger and concentration of industry, there has been a decline of interest in the problem of power exercised by large corporations. Partly this issue has sunk into the background because of prosperity (always a general solvent of social tensions); but principally the reason is that the public has no sense of being exploited. Were this not the case, ambitious politicians would have ferreted out the issue and sought to use it to gain personal advancement (say, by promising stricter laws against collusion if elected).

Theoretically, the existence of a small number of large firms in an economy could well lead to higher prices and a lower volume of sales: there is, after all, no reason why interdependent oligopolists should not behave like the monopoly that they (collectively) are. Yet apparently, at least in the American context, they have for some reason chosen not to exploit the community. Thus, while 'in principle the American is controlled, livelihood and soul, by the large corporation', nonetheless 'in practice he seems not to be completely enslaved'.[1]

The reason is countervailing power. It is true that in many industries there is insufficient competition on the *same* side of the market (i.e. among alternative sellers or buyers of a particular commodity), either because of monopoly power or because of collusion (tacit or overt) between a small number of large organisations. But it is also true that, in the modern economy, much effective restraint on private power arises on the *opposite* side of the market (i.e. not on the part of competitors at all, but of customers to whom one sells and of suppliers from whom one buys). In other words, the real constraint on the power of a strong seller is often the presence in the market of a strong buyer, and vice versa. Oligopsony faces oligopoly and the interests of the community are defended by the balance of power.

Moreover, this balance of power is not accidental: strong buyers develop *as a result* of the existence of strong sellers, and the two groups grow together, neutralising each other, holding each other in check. Original power is hence self-correcting as it generates itself the curb on its own abuse: 'Power on one side of a market creates both the need for, and the prospect of reward to, the exercise of countervailing power from the other side. This means that, as a common rule, we can rely on countervailing power to appear as a curb on economic power.'[2] Original power is an incentive to the powerless to defend themselves, and at the same time an attractive and lucrative bastion to storm. The powerless, in other words, are driven to acquire countervailing power both for their own protection and because of the lure of excess profits to tap.

To illustrate the importance of countervailing power in the American economy, Galbraith offers three examples.

(a) The labour market

Here Galbraith makes the following observation:

> The economic power that the worker faced in the sale of his labour – the competition of many sellers dealing with few buyers – made it necessary that he organize for his own protection. . . . As a general though not invariable rule one finds the strongest unions in the United States where markets are served by large corporations. . . . By contrast there is not a single union of any consequence in American agriculture, the country's closest approach to the competitive model.[3]

The strongest unions are typically found to coexist with the strongest employers. The reasons are both the carrot and the stick. The carrot in large-scale enterprise is high profits, resulting from market power, in which the worker can share once he has strengthened his bargaining position. The stick is the power which large employers have over their (relatively immobile) employees. This latter point is borne out by the fact that the only area of American agriculture where there have been attempts (despite great difficulties) at the organisation of labour has been where large farmers exist and consequently exercise power over their labour-force.

The juxtaposition of strong unions and strong employers means conflict between labour and capital over relative shares. Such conflict, however, is not Marxian class-conflict but the simple and functional conflict of interest that arises between opponents in any market situation. Indeed, the greater threat to the economy appears not to be the presence of this conflict but its absence, as is the case in a period of inflation when unions and corporations make common cause and pass higher wage costs on to the consumer.

(b) Retailing

A misleading (if harmless) simplification in economic theory is to argue as if the producers of consumer goods sell their products directly to final consumers (who, of course, being numerous but scattered, lack power). In fact, those producers sell via retailers, and it is large retailing chains which 'are required by their situation to develop countervailing power on the consumer's behalf'.[4] It is clear that without these food chains, cooperative buying networks, department-store chains, mail-order houses, 'the lot of the consumer would be an unhappy one'.[5]

The large retailer is richly rewarded if he can develop market power sufficient to force down the prices he pays to his suppliers, but the exercise of such countervailing power only makes sense if the producers have original power and are guilty of an abuse in the first place: 'The opportunity to exercise such power exists only when the suppliers are enjoying something that can be taken away; i.e., when they are enjoying the fruits of market power from which they can be separated.'[6] A large food retailer, for example, can attempt to obtain lower prices from a giant corporation by threatening to go into production of food products itself if a discount is not forthcoming, but it can reap no comparable benefit when buying staple products directly from the farmer, since the latter has no excess gains to surrender.

Consider the following historical example of how a retailing chain successfully used its power to countervail that of a large oligoplist:

> The rubber tyre industry is a fairly commonplace example of oligopoly. Four large firms are dominant in the market. In the thirties, Sears, Roebuck and Co. was able, by exploiting its role as a large and indispensable customer, to procure tyres from Goodyear Tyre and Rubber Company at a price from twenty-nine to forty per cent lower than the going market. These it resold to thrifty motorists for from a fifth to a quarter less than the same tyres carrying the regular Goodyear brand.[7]

The point here is that the discount was offered not simply because of the well-known economies that result from large-scale bulk buying. It was offered because the retailer had power, and could threaten the producer with loss of custom (as where the retailer either produces the good himself or switches patronage to another supplier) or indeed attract him with seductive benefits (as where the retailer guarantees future markets or agrees to share or take over advertising costs). Such a process, moreover, has an unexpected latent function. The large retailer has power because he represents a huge share of the producer's market, but the spillover often extends to smaller firms as well: clearly, the supplier 'must frequently, in addition, make a partial surrender to less potent buyers if he is not to be more than ever in the power of his large customers'.[8]

We have seen that retailers are able to bid away excess profits from the producers, their suppliers, and have noted Galbraith's view that these gains are passed on by the retailer to the public at large. Galbraith believes that retail chains 'by proxy are the public's main line of defence against the market power of those who produce or process consumers' goods.'[9] He further believes that in America 'chain stores are approximately as efficient in the exercise of countervailing power as a cooperative would be',[10] and that the reason why consumer cooperatives have not developed in America (in contrast to Britain and Scandinavia) is simply that retailing chains were first on the scene and fulfill the same function of defending final consumers against the depredations of producers. The reason for the failure of consumer cooperatives to develop is thus economic rather than ideological: there is nothing in the American personality to prevent collective enterprise, as the example of successful agricultural supply cooperatives indicates.

Galbraith's assertion that retailing chains exercise countervailing power on behalf of the consumer is unfortunately not without ambiguity. The problem here is that, while it is probably true that large retailers do bid some excess profit away from large suppliers (in a manner that small shopkeepers or merchants could not), it is not clear why these giant buyers should necessarily pass their gains on to the consumer. Consumers, after all, lack organisation and have no countervailing power to exert *vis-à-vis* the retailer. Galbraith, at different stages in his career, has adopted three different positions with respect to this ambiguity.

First, in the original edition of *American Capitalism*, he argued as if, since the modern corporation aims at growth of sales rather than maximisation of profit, it would take advantage of a reduction in costs to reduce prices and thereby to expand business. He added, however, that this effect only operates in a period of buoyancy when economy and market are growing (which implies in turn that in a static situation the retailer would have less incentive to pass on gains in the form of lower prices).

Second, in his address to the Washington meeting of the American Economic Association in 1954 (and in the second edition of *American Capitalism*) he announced that the real reason why retailers pass on to the consumer the gains that arise from the exercise of countervailing power is quite simply the rivalry of one retailer with another. In other words, it is competition on the same side of the market (combined with the possibility of new entry if firms make windfall profits) that explains why the consumer benefits via lower prices from the existence of countervailing power: 'My critics have suggested that it is because retailing, the mass buyers notwithstanding, is still a competitive industry. (It is likely to remain one, for entry is almost inherently easy.) I suspect they are right.'[11]

Third, in 1973, apparently increasingly aware of the powerlessness of the consumer, he implied that competition between retailers might not after all be adequate to defend the interests of the shopper: 'When power becomes part of our system, so does Ralph Nader. We are prepared for the explosion of concern now called consumerism. If the consumer is the ultimate source of authority, his abuse is an occasional fault. He cannot be fundamentally at odds with an economic system that he commands. But if the producing firm has comprehensive power and purposes of its own, there is every likelihood of conflict.'[12] The reference to the consumer movement is a clear recommendation that, if the welfare of the ultimate consumer is to be guaranteed, those consumers must band together in unions and representative bodies in order directly to ensure themselves countervailing power.

(c) Agriculture

The small farmer buys from and sells to firms with market power, but his own individual power is nil: one small farmer could withdraw from the market entirely or substantially increase his output without having any impact at all on prices. His misfortune is to be a perfect competitor compelled to trade with large and powerful organisations (suppliers such as insurance companies and manufacturers of farm machinery; customers such as milk-distributors and canneries). His good luck is to have acquired countervailing power. In the USA in 1929 the Federal Farm Board was established and it undertook to sponsor and capitalise a system of national agricultural cooperatives for marketing of output and purchase of input. Again, subsidies were offered, as were quotas, loans, and price and sales guarantees. In all of these ways the government contributed to the essential task of reinforcing the bargaining power of the small farmer.

An alternative to the creation of countervailing power would have been a curb on original power. Agrarian discontent in the form of Granger and Populist movements focused on alleged exploitation of the farmer by railways, trading firms and industrial enterprises, and some laws were indeed passed to moderate the worst abuses of original power (partly because of the considerable political influence exercised by the agricultural interest). Original power, however, was not destroyed, and this Galbraith praises. It would have been a mere exercise in social nostalgia to attack the tobacco companies, meat-packers or other firms which deal with farmers, via the Anti-Trust Laws: railways, when small, may not be powerful, but they are also not efficient, and the same principle is likely to apply throughout the corporate sector. Rather than limiting original power, the government was wise to encourage the development of countervailing power. Such support to particular under-privileged groups does not reduce national welfare. Indeed, it is the chief domestic function of government in peacetime to help to create countervailing power in the economy in those rare instances where original and countervailing power do not automatically develop simultaneously as a pair.[13] Save where the growth of countervailing power is irregular or incomplete, however, the government can justly remain passive.

Countervailing power, in short, provides a justification for leaving authority over production decisions in private hands, despite the tremendous concentration of economic resources in the giant oligopolies. The point to stress here is the demonstrably good performance of the American economy: a rapid rate of growth and technological advance, a high standard of living and efficiency all represent progress, and the fact that these gains have been passed on to the consumer suggests that countervailing power must have been providing a challenge to original power. Like perfect competition, countervailing power ensures a balance of forces, and leaves scope for pluralism and multiple centres of authority. Then, too, it permits the modern economy to reap the benefits both of large corporations and decentralised decision-making without paying the costs in terms of market domination and exploitation, and without the need for State direction, regulation or expropriation. In the absence of countervailing power, 'private decisions could and presumably would lead to the unhampered exploitation of the public or of workers, farmers, and others who are intrinsically weak as individuals. Such decisions would be a proper object of state interference or would soon so become. This interference is now made unnecessary because those affected by the decisions are able, in effect, to look after themselves.'[14]

This is not intended to be a whitewash of Big Business but a reasoned argument. It will, however, nonetheless appeal to those ideologists among others who favour free private enterprise, for, up to now, 'in resting their case for private authority over production decisions on competition, they have had all the tactical mobility of a rider whose horse has been shot out from under him.'[15]

Naturally, nothing in life is perfect; and it would be misleading to claim that countervailing power allocates resources with maximum social efficiency. Galbraith's claim is more modest, simply that it 'does operate in the right direction': 'When a powerful retail buyer forces down the prices of an industry which had previously been enjoying monopoly returns, the result is larger sales of the product, a larger and broadly speaking a more desirable use of labour, materials, and plant in production. But no one can suppose that this happens with precision.'[16] Countervailing power is a second-best solution, but the textbook alternative of perfect competition is in an era of science and technology no longer available, and the more socialist alternative of increased governmental intervention in the economy was, to the Galbraith of *American Capitalism*, really no alternative at all.

II EVALUATION

The doctrine of countervailing power is compelling and its ideological implications far-reaching. It is, however, open to a number of rather telling criticisms and our task at this stage in the discussion is, as Galbraith would say, to 'put the skunk in the air conditioner'.[17] We will group our points under four headings:

(a) The objectives of countervailing power

It might have been thought, on the basis of the quotations we have previously examined, that Galbraith identifies consumer welfare as the primary aim of countervailing power. It might have been assumed that the function of countervailing power is, in the absence of the invisible hand of perfect competition, to ensure the most nearly optimal allocation of resources and convection of prices that is possible in the situation. In fact, however, and while not denying that these advantageous outcomes may to some extent result, Galbraith tends to regard them as mere by-products. They are not the primary objective of countervailing power. To Galbraith, that objective is, rather unexpectedly, the 'minimization of social tension'.

Galbraith cleared up any residual misunderstandings about his intentions in *American Capitalism* when he addressed the American Economic Association in 1954 and announced: 'American society has not recently been threatened in peacetime (or even in wartime) by a shortage of food. There have been times when the tensions of the farming community were a threat to orderly democratic process. The evolution of countervailing power in the labor market has similarly been a major solvent of tensions in the last half-century. Most would now agree, I think, that this has been worth a considerable price.'[18] The 'considerable price' is misallocation of resources and a slower improvement in average standards of living throughout the community, reminding us that countervailing power may prove an expensive luxury. Still, expensive luxuries can easily be afforded by an affluent society where material goods are abundant and the maximisation of consumer utility has become an obsolete goal. This is just as well, since in a world of countervailing power it is often the consumer who is saddled with the net cost of tranquillity. Galbraith himself points out that in the view of the orthodox, competition-oriented, consumer-oriented tradition in economics, 'the sufficient and only test of social change is whether, assuming organization and technology to be given, it reduces prices to the consumer', and then admits: 'This is not a test which countervailing can always satisfy. The development of such power by workers or farmers may result primarily in a redistribution of returns. It may, by raising marginal costs, raise prices to the consumer.'[19] The point is simply that the consumer is also a citizen and hence still benefits from countervailing power, precisely

because the social serenity and relief of tension that result from a
more equitable distribution of power are productive of more social
satisfaction than would have been the mere consumption of a few
baubles and trinkets more.

Naturally, many observers of the social scene will disagree with
Galbraith as to the relative importance of commodity utility and the
relief of social tension, while many readers of *American Capitalism*
will find it hard to believe that the author's true goal is the latter
rather than the former. It is in any case, however, by no means
proven that countervailing power really acts as a solvent of tensions.
Galbraith argues (and few would disagree) that combination and
cooperative action help individuals to improve their power-
positions by becoming members of blocs or groups. Yet a corporate
state where men face each other as members of large units rather
than on their own could well be characterised by more disagree-
ment rather than less, for when elephants fight, it is not just the grass
that suffers but other elephants as well. And this is particularly likely
to be the case since Galbraith offers no definition of the optimal
allocation of power. There are, after all, a vast number of possible
positions of equilibrium in the power-struggle between two groups;
and one group (say, a trade union) is bound to be eager at all times
to increase its power at the expense of another (say, a corporation)
in order to move to a more agreeable position of inertia.

The acquisition of countervailing power is haphazard and rough-
and-ready, and it is unjustifiably optimistic to expect the force of the
counter-push to be precisely and exactly what is needed to minimise
resentment, insecurity and ill-will. Suppose, for example, that a
large corporation has original power and is able to make monopoly
profits, and that a trade union now obtains countervailing power in
order to share in those profits. Here the bargaining is likely to be
acrimonious (redistribution in the general social interest can be a
painful process, particularly if the union is willing to resort to strike
action) and the final result not indubitably the optimal solvent of
potential social tension: the firm may be forced to give up more than
simply its excess profits (union leaders do not always know a firm's
true profits, nor do they always care) and may bitterly resent the
move from abnormally high to abnormally low returns that
occurred when it was not only faced by countervailing power but
outfaced by it. There is no reason to imagine that countervailing
power will ever be of exactly the right intensity to ensure a true
balance of power in some objective sense, for it is, after all, one thing

to say that countervailing power *opposes* original power and quite another to say that it *neutralises* it. Nor is there any reason to anticipate that, even if some rough set of checks and balances did develop by force of power-parity, such an arbitrary stalemate would be widely acceptable. Social tensions (being subjective and non-rational in nature) might continue to exist, as one group warily eyes the other and plots its future strategy, but such tensions the model is ultimately unable to incorporate, since it is excessively static (it ignores the possibility that the power struggle will escalate along the same lines as the arms race) and, here as elsewhere in Galbraith's work, assumes what it sets out to prove in this case, that both parties to a contract will at some crucial moment in time agree that power is 'correctly' distributed and that each bloc has had a 'fair' deal).

Moving from the microeconomic to the national level, moreover, it appears even more unlikely that social justice will automatically result from a network of relationships having none of the logic behind them either of planned power or of unplanned competition. Nor is it probable that the subjective perception on a national scale of social tension can be dealt with by offering for contemplation the equilibration of the economy via the conflict of organised power groups, of vast monolithic aggregations each locked in his own private struggle. The public consciousness may indeed be shocked by the spectacle of a war between titans, sceptical that a series of partial solutions will add up to general equilibrium, depressed at the sight of the new inequities in income and power which arise, and alarmed by the gaps in a model which fails to explain away at least three important cases of power-imbalance.

The first case refers to the problem of the dual economy. The doctrine of countervailing power presumes that the strong confront the strong. In a dual economy, however, it often happens that the strong confront the weak. A large retailing chain or mighty trade union negotiates with large corporations, but it deals as well with small and relatively powerless firms, and while it may have developed its countervailing power in order to bid away the excess profits of giant organisations, it can also use that power as original power against the natural victim. In the United States, for example, footwear, furnishings and farm produce tend to be produced by small firms working in fairly competitive conditions, and yet are sold to a great extent to chain-store retailing outlets. Tension may well arise in such an unbalanced situation, for there not all actors have equal access to power.

Then, secondly, Galbraith neglects the possible social tensions that might develop *within* a group (say, disagreements over differentials between different grades of labour within a single powerful trade union), and he underplays the concentration of the power of decision-making in the economy that bloc-bargaining represents. In the model, big decisions in big corporations, big unions or big retailing chains are made by a few men (perhaps by one on each side of the bargaining table). This is democratic in the sense that any political power is democratic (where the leaders are elected by secret ballot), or at least represents rule by the meritocracy (where the leaders evolve via appointment and promotion on the basis of past performance). It does mean, however, that a few men have the power to make extremely significant decisions affecting vast numbers, and this fact may in turn lead to tensions, both within society as a whole (as where, say, a single corporate head is known to have taken the decision to shut down a factory and transfer its operations abroad to another part of a multinational corporation) and within the organisation (resentment, for example, on the part of those excluded from the decision-making process).

Finally, thirdly, Galbraith neglects the threat to the community that arises when interests of buyer and seller coincide, when they elect to make common cause and pool their power rather than to use it to neutralise one another. Yet social tensions would more likely be exacerbated than assuaged by, for example, the unedifying spectacle of a strong union and a strong corporation working together to obtain tariff protection via an organised pressure group which in reality is no less than a conspiracy against the consumer. Of course, the conspiracy need not be so transparent, as in the case of a strong union in an industry (oligopolised or perfectly competitive) producing a necessity, a union which now restricts supplies of labour to the producers of the good in order to raise the price of labour. Because the supply of inputs is reduced, the quantity of output falls. Because the good is a necessity, the reduction in quantity supplied is likely to lead to a greater-than-proportionate rise in price, and hence to a rise in profits because of the inelastic demand-curve. The producers themselves could only have engineered such a collective reduction in output by collusive action (and cartels may be illegal) or tacit restraint (which is difficult to administer). They are likely to be grateful to the union for aiding them to reduce quantity supplied and thus to raise prices. The public is likely to be less grateful (as are unions in industries producing luxuries rather than necessities, whose members will in consequence expend relatively more physical and mental energy for a relatively smaller return).

Naturally, the public may be unaware of the implicit conspiracy masquerading in the guise of countervailing power. It may genuinely believe that chain stores counterbalance the power of great producers and genuinely not know that (the former because it produces 'own brands') both are in alliance against the less-organised producers of raw materials. In such a case, a *belief* in countervailing power may help to relieve social tensions quite independent of (indeed, in spite of) the behaviour of countervailing power itself. It is cases such as this which make the reader wonder if countervailing power is really more than simply a dubious defence of non-competitive conditions, Big Business and the corporate state.

(b) The position of the consumer

The fact that the union or the retailing chain succeeds in obtaining a share in the monopoly profits of the large corporation need not mean that the benefits are ever passed on to the consumer. Countervailing power might in practice mean no more than the redistribution of abnormally large gains as between powerful buyers and powerful sellers.

Consumers being a powerless mass, a case could be made out for giving them countervailing power, either through a Ministry of Consumer Protection or through private bodies such as consumer cooperatives. While Galbraith in the 1970s did hint at the need for increased protection, his principal explanation in the immediate post-1954 period of the way in which the benefits from the exercise of countervailing power are transferred to the consumer is to be found in his optimistic account of how competition among giant retailers compels them to pass on the benefits they acquired in their war against giant producers. Quite apart from the confusing reference to consumer welfare (rather than relief of social tensions), this interpretation of events can be challenged from a dual perspective.

First, while it is well known that prices are usually lower in large supermarkets than in small corner stores, the cause of such lower prices is unfortunately less well known and exceptionally difficult empirically to ascertain. It might, of course, be, as Galbraith states, that the large oligopsonist chain successfully bids away the excessive profits of its suppliers and then passes the gains on to the final consumer; but it might also be the fact that the chain simply has economies of large scale in bulk-buying, promotion and retailing. A large firm is more likely to be able to mobilise cash for cash discounts; it saves via the centralisation of accounting and computational facilities on behalf of a multitude of branches; it is able to spread risks over a number of lines of goods; and it benefits from more rapid turnover caused by the attractions to customers of a wider range of items available in multiples compared with smaller shops. Clearly, chain stores have considerable advantages in selling and merchandising, and the lower prices they offer cannot therefore be taken as *prima facie* evidence of gains arising specifically from countervailing power.

Second, it is not clear why such gains as result from size should not be retained by the seller but shared with the buyer. The big retailers might, after all, collude, or at least enter into some tacit agreement on how best to deal with the dangers of interdependence. It would be surprising if they did not resort to measures such as price leadership or simply a policy of price rigidity in an effort to minimise their uncertainty, and yet such practices not only protect inefficiency by restricting competition but allow retailers to increase profit-margins excessively through the device of keeping selling prices fixed at a time when costs are falling (perhaps due to exercise of power). Indeed, restrictive practices could even mean reduced total quantity sold, higher prices to the consumer and (depending on the elasticity of demand) higher profits.

Of course, Galbraith asserts that profits are not the overriding objective of the corporation, which is more likely to attempt to maximise the rate of growth of its sales subject to financial and security constraints. It is, however, important to remember that in Galbraith's model the typical giant attempts to grow not so much via a reduction in prices as through advertising and the manipulation of consumer demand. The giant may seek to sell a greater quantity of output at the same or even a higher price, and in this case benefits arising from the exercise of countervailing power may be wasted (at least in part) on sales effort rather than passed on in the form of lower prices. Clearly, a powerful retailer could in one way or another deploy his forces against rather than on behalf of the consumer, should he wish to do so.

(c) The inevitability thesis

Galbraith believes that the economy in most cases retains the autoregulative properties of the liberal model precisely because the existence of original power itself is likely to generate equal and opposite countervailing power. It is, however, by no means true that original power dependably begets compensating power to counterbalance itself, or that oligopoly typically engenders oligopsony. The fact is that power need not arise in pairs.

Despite Galbraith's assertion that the birth of countervailing power is no adventitious or accidental occurrence, there is in the real world little evidence of firms deliberately growing large purely or principally in order to acquire countervailing power. Retailing chains, it is true, have developed at the same time as the giant manufacturing corporations. Association, however, is no proof of causation: as we have seen, economies of scale in bulk-buying or organisation would adequately account for the success of the chain store in selling at lower prices, quite apart from its presumed ability to exercise market power. Of course, in a situation of imperfect competition, the large firm does acquire such power. The point we are making is simply that such power appears more likely than not to be only another by-product of those economies of scale that led to large size, and that the objective of the growth of the chain-store was not specifically to develop countervailing power *vis-à-vis* a clearly perceived locus of original power.

Alex Hunter has considered the operation of bargaining power in producers' goods industries (a case which Galbraith mentions but, preferring to concentrate on markets for consumer goods and labour, does not explore), and reaches similar conclusions, namely that in these markets countervailing power is often present and yet an unintended outcome nonetheless. Thus, while the car industry is concentrated, that concentration can adequately be explained by economies of large scale without reliance on the need to confront a concentrated tyre industry (tyres hardly representing a substantial percentage of the cost of a car). And while the National Health Service is in Britain indubitably the main customer of the giant pharmaceutical companies, it is absurd to account for socialised medicine in terms of some desire to cream off the benefits arising from original power rather than in terms of general political, social and philosophical considerations. The implications are clear, that one cannot expect a coalition of the weak spontaneously and inevitably to develop in order to oppose the strong; and that countervailing power, while useful, is, in its incidence, 'erratic and unpredictable'.[20]

In some cases countervailing power has developed and yet still failed to act as a dependable regulatory mechanism. Galbraith optimistically asserts, for example, that the British cooperative movement has exercised the same sort of pressure on behalf of the consumer as the giant retailing chain in America. Hunter, however, has convincingly demonstrated that 'the movement, rather than exploiting an advantageous position, has, on the contrary, neglected its opportunities for exercising countervailing power'.[21] The cooperatives have been reluctant to move out of food and household stores into newer lines, such as consumer durables. They invest as much as 75 per cent of their available capital *outside* the movement (a very conservative approach to liquidity, explicable partly in terms of the fact that consumers' shares are withdrawable upon demand). They indulge in little price-cutting, and prefer to sell their products at going market prices (as determined by their private enterprise competitors), passing the benefits back to the shareholder in the form of dividends. They have willingly sold branded goods at maintained retail prices in the past without protesting to producers about this infringement of competitive freedom, and passive acceptance has unquestionably favoured resale price maintenance. They have failed to penetrate concentrated industries and protect the consumer by underselling private producers (rather a surprise since the movement possesses guaranteed retail outlets). Here we have a case of sleepy countervailing power, for it is clear from Hunter's evidence that the cooperatives have, at least in the past, hardly fought very intensively on behalf of the public against the might of Big Business (which, Galbraith believes, first called them into existence).

The growth of countervailing power being 'erratic and unpredictable', it is understandable that history provides many examples of cases where push failed to stimulate counter-push. One of these we have already mentioned: in a dual economy, the countervailing power that the retailing chain exercises against the original power of the manufacturing giant may well appear as uncountervailed original power to the myriads of dwarfs from whom it also purchases and who remain powerless. Another example of the failure of countervailing power to develop is to be found in the labour market. Galbraith says: 'In the ultimate sense it was the power of the steel industry, not the organizing abilities of John L. Lewis and Philip Murray, that brought the United Steel Workers into being.'[22] What he fails to mention is that some 35 years elapsed between the creation of 'original power' (the foundation of the United States Steel Corporation) and the birth of 'countervailing power' (the organisation of a strong union, the United Steel Workers). This long gestation period suggests that concentration was not after all the cause of unionisation and that *post hoc* was evidently not *propter hoc* (not even, as Galbraith so ambiguously puts it, 'in the ultimate sense'). More generally, his contention that strong unions are normally only found in those markets inhabited by strong corporations is simply incorrect, and he also neglects the fact that nowadays many a union veils more power than it counters and constitutes a new locus of original power in its own right.

Galbraith himself gives examples of cases where countervailing power has not inevitably and automatically developed, and praises the State intervention that has resulted in such circumstances in order to buttress a weak bargaining position (witness farm price support, or government aid to set up a new marketing cooperative or trade union). He himself thus admits that the balance of power need not necessarily arise as a result of forces operating spontaneously in the market and introduces normative overtones into the discussion by declaring that the government *ought to* help the weak to acquire power-parity.

He introduces normative overtones but provides inadequate guide-lines for the policy-maker in a confusing area where redistribution of power is also redistribution of income and where value-judgements are inescapable. This is a major omission since, because the declared aim of countervailing power is minimisation of social tension rather than maximisation of *per capita* commodity consumption, the norms governing intervention are not likely in his view to be purely economic: social justice in the form of a more acceptable distribution of the national income is as valid a goal as efficiency or competitive pricing. Moreover, having countenanced social direction in markets where countervailing power is completely absent, it is surprising Galbraith remains reluctant to conceive of it in markets where countervailing power is present but non-optimal. It is surprising, in other words, that he continues to think in terms of on/off rather than fine tuning.

To make matters still more complex, government support to the countervailing power of the disadvantaged is, in the Galbrathian world, neither automatic nor spontaneous. Indeed, it appears only forthcoming when the weak have already formed themselves into some sort of pressure-group. As Galbraith puts it: 'In the actual sequence of events, some measure of organization by the group themselves must precede any very important government subsidy to their developing market power.'[23] Hence the first Anti-Trust Act was a response to the Granger Movement, the second came after the election success of the New Freedom Movement, and the third was an answer to the successful lobby of small businessmen in the New Deal era for protection from large firms.

The point seems to be that State aid to support the power of a group often depends on that group already having power; and thus that the State is more likely to support the strongest and most vocal among the disadvantaged while leaving the weakest in the shadows of oblivion. Consider the case of the workers: 'The trade unions have sought and won a legal climate basically favorable to themselves. In the industrial states – Michigan, Pennsylvania, New York – where the political power of workers is greatest, their success has also been greatest.'[24] And the more depressing case of the farmers: 'Of late, American farmers have not been satisfied with the support that the government has accorded to their bargaining position. In recent decades farmers have shrunk from a large to a comparatively small political minority, for while our population has been increasing rapidly, the number of farmers has been showing an absolute decline.'[25]

Workers and farmers are to Galbraith disadvantaged groups. If, however, pressure groups are more likely to prevail with government the more power they have, then it is certainly possible that privileged groups (and not the disadvantaged at all) will, having maximum strength, enjoy maximum influence. After all, large groups put pressure not only on each other but on politicians as well, and may seek to use the State to enhance their power still further by lobbying for laws favourable to their own special interest. The small firm is seldom able to win the ear of executive or legislative in the way that, say, a large multinational or a huge trade union is able to do, and this may lead to economic and social imbalance.

Government support, by strengthening one group against another, is likely to be self-feeding, once we realise that economic power gives a group political power and makes it a likely candidate for still more economic power. Naturally, Galbraith hopes that the government will recognise the needs of the silent, the powerless and the dispossessed, but his own references to the pressures of the lobby make one wonder how much influence it is possible to exercise without the previous possession of economic power. It does not, in any case, appear desirable for pressure-groups and interest-blocs to have quite so much influence in a democratic society.

Of course, Galbraith might optimistically be presuming that one group will in the political market as well countervail another, thereby guaranteeing a balance of power based on a balance of influence. This might be the situation where big retailers are lobbying for the abolition of resale price maintenance while simultaneously big manufacturers are lobbying for its retention. It might also be the case where an employers' federation is pressing for measures to restrict trade unions while unions are simultaneously pressing for an extension of their powers. It might be the case – but, then again, it might not be.

(d) Inflation and integration

Galbraith admits that countervailing power can be neutralised by inflation and circumvented by vertical integration, but in *American Capitalism* seems to regard both these phenomena as exceptional rather than commonplace. In a world characterised by both these phenomena, however, even Galbraith would accept that the doctrine of countervailing power loses much of its relevance.

Consider first inflation. Clearly, 'If buyers are plentiful – if supply is small in relation to current demand – sellers are under no compulsion to surrender to the bargaining power of any particular customer.'[26] Where the level of demand is high, the balance of power is upset: 'The market power of strong sellers, until now offset by that of strong buyers, is enhanced. The countervailing power of weak sellers is suddenly and adventitiously reinforced.'[27] In a buoyant economy, a strong union demands higher pay, and this the employer readily concedes since he is able to pass the additional costs on to the consumer in the form of higher prices. Rather than counterbalancing one another, union and corporation in a period of inflation enter into an alliance, a monolithic conspiracy against the public. In a buoyant economy, in other words, the question of conflict is shelved (or, rather, the burden of resentment is transferred from powerful unions to powerless consumers) but the need then arises for a new kind of countervailing power: State intervention in the form of prices and incomes policy to defend the public interest, which has figured prominently in Galbraith's work since *American Capitalism*.

From Galbraith's own examples it is fair to conclude that, historically speaking, most arrangements for the exercise of counter-vailing power in the labour-market have developed in periods of depression. It is, however, an odd doctrine which makes depression typical, full employment an irrelevant exception (not least because it ignores the possibility, widely discussed in the 1950s, that successful attempts on the part of unions to resist cuts in real wages could lead to a return of pre-war underemployment equilibrium). The theory is, in short, not valid in all macroeconomic environments, and evidently not particularly applicable in our own times.

Consider now the case of vertical integration. Here the danger is that 'there are producers of consumers' goods who have protected themselves from exercise of countervailing power. Some, like the automobile and the oil industry, have done so by integrating their distribution through to the consumer – a strategy which attests the importance of the use of countervailing power by retailers. Others have found it possible to maintain dominance over an organization of small and dependent and therefore fairly powerless dealers.'[28] Fortunately for the shopper, in general 'most positions of market power in the production of consumers' goods are covered by positions of countervailing power.'[29]

We have already seen that a huge buyer (say, a chain store) can threaten to integrate backward into the production of the good, should his supplier be reluctant to share excessive profits. We ought now to note too that the seller can also threaten to integrate forward and sell direct to the final consumer, thereby circumventing a troublesome retailer. Naturally, such threats to seek alternative sources of supply via 'own brands' or to seek alternative outlets may be no more than the usual process of bluff and counter-bluff that accompanies any bargain. But the threat to duplicate, in order to be meaningful, implies the power to duplicate; and if A integrates forwards while B integrates backwards, the net result is not the countervailing power of strong seller *vis-à-vis* strong buyer but the co-existence of two giant integrated monoliths, debating whether to compete or to collude.

Galbraith's approach to integration and power tends to leave one question unanswered, and it is of great importance: if the retailer himself can so easily enter production, then why should there not already have been new entrants in the form of new manufacturers, particularly those whose existing lines are not too different from the new product (for surely expansion from biscuits into bread is easier than integration backwards from retailing to baking)? If, in other words, the mass distributor can so easily attack the privileged position of an existing producer, then surely other manufacturers can successfully to do as well. And if this is the case, then the whole doctrine of countervailing power seems an unnecessary burden. Galbraith might just as well have said that high profits tend to get bid away by new entrants and more intensive competition. This result is not unknown even to orthodox economists.

We have argued in this chapter that a number of objections may be raised to Galbraith's theory of countervailing power. We have seen that countervailing power is unlikely to attain either the objective of tension-minimisation or that of welfare-maximisation; that original power does not inevitably generate just adequate countervailing power (and that the State does not inevitably just adequately fill the gap); and that the theory insufficiently incorporates inflation and integration, two of the most significant features of the modern economy. We have implied that Galbraith was wrong to explain the successful performance of the American economy in terms of power and answering power rather than in terms of the market and a modified price mechanism (despite the existence of large corporations and the undeniable absence from so many markets of perfect competition).

In his writings after *American Capitalism*, Galbraith makes no mention of countervailing power, and in *The New Industrial State* moves even further away from the idea of competitive markets by postulating a planned economy, at least in the powerful corporate sector. He goes further, and says that blocs (unions, retailers, the government, the corporations) actually work together to promote each other's growth and security rather than quarrelling over relative shares. He conspicuously neglects the the opportunity to say that two technostructures exert countervailing power against one another, and argues that they cooperate by contract, while completely ignoring the hard bargaining that must have determined the terms of that agreement.

Galbraith's approach has changed. Continuity, however, exists, in so far as Galbraith retains his tendency to see men as parts of blocs, and still sees social justice and equilibrium in terms of a balance of power between these blocs. In the era of the corporate state, the power of the individual remains, in his view, inseparable from the power of the group.

5 The Satisfaction of Wants

The case for economic growth traditionally reposes in substantial measure on the presumed satisfaction of authentic consumer desires. Galbraith writes: 'That social progress is identical with a rising standard of living has the aspect of a faith. No society has ever before provided such a high standard of living as ours, hence none is as good.'[1]

This is, however, a faith which Galbraith rejects for a reason which forms the subject of this chapter and is as follows: present-day preference patterns are not authentic to the consumer but the result of manipulation by the producer.

In Section I we will examine the relationship between manipulation and the goals of the technostructure; and in Section II the significance of manipulation for the liberal theory of consumers and markets. In Section III we shall attempt to evaluate the extent and importance of consumer manipulation, and to assess its relevance to the case for economic growth.

I MANIPULATION AND THE TECHNOSTRUCTURE

The large firm, as we have already seen, cannot simply dump its products on to the market, but must both forecast future market demand and seek to influence it through its sales strategies. The large firm assigns great importance to the ability to manage and tailor consumer responses in accordance with its needs (for income) and its plans (for outlay) since, because of the technological imperative, it cannot risk dependence on unpredictable and uncertain market signals.

The techniques utilised for this purpose are well known, and include sophisticated market research (to find out what the consumer can be persuaded to buy, and at what price), consumer-credit schemes (to give the purchaser additional means of payment), product design, packaging and technological innovation.

Advertising strategies play a particularly important role in conditioning the consumer to want a specific product (often instilling in him a desire for the commodity through an appeal to emulation or the stimulation of psychological needs involving status, power, aggression, virility and femininity, even national pride), and television advertising most of all: the latter allows of persuasion with no minimum standard of literacy or intelligence.

In Chapter 2 we saw that the technostructure has three goals of its own, namely job-satisfaction through technological virtuosity, security and growth. It will be helpful to consider the technostructure's relationship with the final consumer under the same three headings.

First, technological virtuosity. Innovation indubitably increases the job-satisfaction of the experts. It also has the function of stimulating demand: the popular view that newest is best and the universal esteem in which scientific progress is held both facilitate successful persuasion.

In practice, spurious model changes (e.g. longer cars with bigger tail-fins), continuous product development (often leading to a high failure rate where changes are made before engineers have had time to iron out existing wrinkles), planned obsolescence, all may be undesirable from the point of view of the consumer. They can, however, be good selling points and hence essential for the technostructure: not only do changes and inventions provide a challenge to the technologist, but they also contribute to the growth and security of the corporation and its staff. Were goods made to last, were they reliable and sturdy rather than shoddy, they would require less frequent replacement; and this in turn would narrow the market for the output of the firm (particularly since the typical enterprise Galbraith has in mind is, as we have indicated, not extensively diversified) and retard its expansion. Fortunately for the technocrat, product development does take place and is made vendable through advertising: 'To create the demand for new cars we must contrive elaborate and functionless changes each year and then subject the consumer to ruthless psychological pressures to persuade him of their importance. Were this process to falter or break down, the consequences would be disturbing.'[2]

The test of a 'successful' innovation is evidently not whether it truly improves human welfare (indeed, an innovation may be rejected because, although socially desirable, it is too technical to become part of the firm's image or play its part in the firm's sales strategy). Nor is it the satisfaction of genuine human needs (product development typically precedes consumer response, and cannot therefore be justified in terms of consumer sovereignty). The test of a 'successful' innovation is simply whether it adds to sales: 'In the planning system . . . the test of innovation is not need but what can be sold – or what serves in the management of individual or public demand. In the case of consumers' goods a change that is without function may be as serviceable for selling a product as a change that has function.'[3]

The technostructure clearly has economic as well as technological goals in so far as innovation is not just a game for graduates but an aid to expansion of sales. The technocrat can neither indulge in spurious innovation for its own sake nor direct his technological virtuosity into developments which benefit the public but not the corporation; and his goal of job-satisfaction is distinctly constrained by the imperative of saleability of output. Fortunately, the very presence of a scientist in the works is itself a marketable novelty, so great is the present-day prestige of research and development (particularly when that research and development has been magnified through merchandising strategies).

Second, security. Mass production presupposes mass consumption, and advertising and salesmanship help to guarantee that quantitatively and qualitatively demand will be forthcoming.

In the orthodox neo-classical 'accepted sequence' of the elementary economics textbook, the individual communicates his desires to the market and the market transmits this information to the producer. Such a transmission mechanism may still obtain in the 'market system'; but in the 'planning system' there exists a 'revised sequence' according to which the producer first decides on the good he wishes to produce, the quantity he wishes to sell (in the light of his security and growth objectives) and the price at which he wishes to sell it, and then manipulates consumer demand until he secures the desired response. In short, if the firm is to plan ahead it must be able in due course to bend the consumer to its needs, to impose corporate targets on individual shoppers. Here Galbraith is standing conventional economics on its head: the public, he is asserting, is now serving industry rather than industry serving the public, since nowadays production comes first and wants are artificially generated after the event.

Advertising and salesmanship help to attract new customers to a promoted product and away from both non-promoted activities (such as savings and leisure) and non-promoted products (such as those originating in the competitive market system). This means that sales promotion is not a zero-sum game (in the sense of a game played to reallocate a fixed quantity of consumer spending on a given commodity) but actually increases demand for that commodity as a whole and thus provokes some redistribution in the national income to the detriment of the weak. For this reason Galbraith rejects the view that in oligopolistic conditions corporations only neutralise and cancel out one another's sales campaigns: were advertising mere waste, he comments, then 'steps would long ago have been taken to limit advertising outlays by common agreement'.[4] The fact that this has not happened suggests that all who advertise do in fact derive benefit from this form of competition. Put in simple terms, what Galbraith is saying is this: an advertisement for a Ford car is an advertisement for a car as well as a Ford, and is likely to increase total demand for genus as well as species.

Note, however, that advertising and salesmanship are not intended to attract new customers to a particular brand to the detriment of a competitor. Traditional economic theory teaches that, in conditions of oligopoly, firms will institute administered and relatively rigid price-levels to minimise the risk of sanguinary price-wars, and will instead compete via publicity and product differentiation (real or imaginary). Galbraith, as we have seen, goes one step further and argues that the technostructures of giant corporations do not compete at all, but make contracts. This is partly because they are not profit-maximisers, partly because of their conviction that all firms in an industry must expand simultaneously or not at all: 'Given the goals of the technostructure all firms will seek to expand sales. Each, accordingly, must seek to do so if it is not to lose out to others. Out of this effort, from firms that are fully able to play the game, comes a crude equilibrating process which accords to each participant a reasonably reliable share of the market.'[5] A corporation losing sales to another will adapt its sales strategy until it is successful in restoring its previous share; but a new sales formula is never used in anger, only in self-defence, to promote security and facilitate planning.

Third, growth. Production presupposes consumption, and expanding production presupposes expanding consumption. The corporation cannot grow if purchasers for its products are not forthcoming, but want-creation dependably keeps the level of demand not only high but growing.

A textbook Keynesian would associate high savings with high incomes. Galbraith, however, argues that such a view is unrealistic and static: the household does not serve the corporation through frugality and the provision of savings but through the purchase of output, and advertising, by making such consumption seem an index of social merit, standing, achievement, ecstasy, is able to shift the consumption function upwards over time, in accordance with the growth objective of the technostructure.

At the same time, by making goods seem important, salesmanship not only stimulates the individual to spend a higher percentage of a given income but also to expand his earnings. Insatiability is essential to the growth-objective of the technostructure; leisure-preference and targeted levels of consumption are anathema. If people were allowed to satisfy their desires for commodities and simple services at some low level of income, then they would at that point stop both earning and spending. The technostructure, however, has been able to frustrate these natural impulses and to engender, purely in its own interest, a revolution of rising expectations that makes rising living standards appear of vital importance. The proof that the technostructure has succeeded in creating the kind of populus it requires is as follows: 'In 1939 the real income of employed workers in the United States was very nearly the highest on record and it was then the highest of any country in the world. In the next quarter century it doubled. Had the 1939 income been a terminal objective, work effort would have been cut in half in the ensuing twenty-five years. In fact, there was a slight increase in weekly hours actually worked. This was a remarkable achievement.'[6] Want-creation today plays the same role as the Protestant Ethic in a previous era, that of repressing idleness and promoting overtime. The difference is that want-creation also implies that private thrift is waste (as indeed it is from the point of view of the technostructure, with a pool of internally generated corporate funds at its disposal).

A society which evaluates its performance by its standard of living will tend to view its citizens in the same way, and hence commodity-consumption becomes an index of prestige. This, combined with social mobility, builds an inflationary bias into the system: inflationary claims 'are progressively enhanced by the progressively more classless character of consumption – by the increasing unwillingness of any large group in the society to believe that it was meant by nature to have less.'[7] Moreover, since the prestige of production produces the prestige of the producer, advertising, by making saleable goods appear important and business indispensable for welfare, promotes the social standing of the technostructure. Naturally, 'if increased production ceased to be of prime importance, the needs of the industrial system would no longer be accorded automatic priority'.[8]

In summary then, we have seen in this section an illustration of the 'Principle of Consistency', a demonstration of how the technostructure by the skillful use of a vast and subtle public relations mechanism has succeeded in imposing its goals on the community. The technostructure has adapted belief to its needs, both with respect to the purchase of individual commodities and with respect to the importance of production as a whole. It has induced a high valuation of innovation, security and growth. It has brought about a reduction in the average propensity to save and caused leisure to be despised. It has made the labour-force reliable in a way that it would not have been 'in the absence of pressure to purchase the next car or to meet the payments on the last'.[9] It has moulded the kind of man needed by the modern mature corporation and has caused him to neglect goals more truly in the national interest than its own. It has, in short, imposed a planned economy. As Galbraith says:

> The most meaningful distinction between a market and a planned economy, so it seems to me, turns on whether and to what extent accommodation is to producer or consumer choice. The more responsive the producer must be to consumer choice, the more it is a market economy. The greater his power to establish prices and to persuade, command or otherwise arrange the consumer response at these prices, the more it is a planned economy. Intervention by the state does not alter the fact of planning; it changes only its nature, extent or efficacy.[10]

An important and socially deleterious by-product of planning via consumer manipulation is inequality between the sexes and the conversion of women into a crypo-servant class. Such inequality was not expressly designed by sexist male chauvinist pigs in order to oppress the female of the species, and must be treated as a social superstructure arising from a particular economic basis: consuming is paramount and potential domestic servants prefer well-paid jobs outside the home, leaving women with no alternative but to sacrifice their careers in order to adminster commodity consumption. Here as usual ideology follows economic necessity and reinforces it: thus the 'Convenient Social Virtue'[11] (which ascribes social merit to the performance of underpaid and menial tasks essential to the well-being of the powerful) approves of the woman who is a good home-maker and does not sacrifice her correct womanly values to the chimera of a full-time job, a choice which she is made to regard as shockingly irresponsible.

As a result, the educated woman in the modern industrial society tends to exercise her mind largely by acting as an intelligent shopper. She chooses between different consumer goods, allocates family budgets, runs an elaborate home, arranges for the maintenance of complex household equipment, manages social occasions, transports and stores goods, cooks meals. Naturally, labour-saving consumer durables (e.g. the washing machine or the vacuum cleaner) do exist to help her perform her household duties, and this fact favours both the market system and the planning system. It favours the market system since small-scale service industries spring up to keep these durables in good repair. It favours the planning system since large corporations tend to provide equipment and spare parts to the service industries, and also because the process of innovation and the credo that newer means better causes such durables to be replaced at frequent intervals.

Without the willingness of women to stay at home and administer consumption, the present economic order would be severely hampered in its ability to expand; and the sacrifice of women's life-opportunities must be weighed at the margin against the alleged benefits resulting from expanded production and consumption of material commodities. The social cost in terms of human unhappiness can naturally not be quantified. What we do know, however, is that the economic value of housewives' services (not included in GNP statistics since it represents unpaid activity) would probably, if included, boost American figures by as much as 25 per cent.[12]

The present system, Galbraith believes, is unfair to women, since it offers the housewife the sensation of morally commendable behaviour as a poor substitute for pecuniary payment and job-satisfaction. Moreover, it means that women within the household are not on an equal basis with men: the man is the head of the family by virtue of his earning power, while the woman is an unpaid servant who performs the tasks and duties assigned to her. In the modern household, it is the woman who must subordinate her preferences to those of her husband, with respect to level of expenditure (determined by his income), style of expenditure (determined by his position) and choice of locality (determined by his job). Such subordination leads Galbraith to dismiss the tendency of economists to speak of the 'household' as a fiction which blinds them to the need to disaggregate: in reality, he argues, 'the household, in the established economics, is essentially a disguise for the exercise of male authority'.[13]

Galbraith finds this situation unacceptable: 'The notion that economic society requires something approaching half of its adult members to accept subordinate status is not easily defended'.[14] The time has come for women, like all other puppets manipulated by the technostructure, to 'perceive their role as instruments for expanding consumption on behalf of the planning system'.[15]

II MANIPULATION AND ECONOMIC THEORY

Galbraith believes that the orthodox theory of consumer desires rests upon two fundamental but fallacious postulates:

(a) The postulate of non-satiety, that 'the urgency of wants does not diminish appreciably as more of them are satisfied or, to put the matter more precisely, to the extent that this happens it is not demonstrable.'[16] In other words, once man has satisfied his physical needs (for food, clothing, shelter), their place is taken by psychologically based needs, whose extent is virtually infinite. Because all needs are unlikely ever to be fully satisfied, the orthodox economist postulates scarce means confronted by a multiplicity of ends.

(b) The postulate of independence of wants, that 'wants originate in the personality of the consumer or, in any case . . . they are given data for the economist. The latter's task is merely to seek their satisfaction. He has no need to inquire how these wants are formed. His function is sufficiently fulfilled by maximising the goods that supply the wants.'[17]

These two postulates enable orthodox economic theory to regard the GNP as an index of welfare, and to identify an increasing supply of goods and services with increasing felicity. The proof is consumer sovereignty: in a free society, if the individual consumer does not want the goods on offer, he has the right to demand others or to substitute leisure for work. Wants are demonstrably insatiable, and this piece of empirical evidence may be treated as the justification for economic growth.

Galbraith, however, rejects both postulates of economic orthodoxy:

(a) Economists have long recognised that incremental units of a commodity yield progressively less satisfaction (or 'utility') to the consumer, but have shied away from applying the concept of diminishing marginal utility to the incremental consumption of all commodities taken together as a group. Galbraith regards this inconsistency as a failing and finds it eminently reasonable that, the greater the aggregate consumption of the individual, the less will be the additional satisfaction he derives from still more.

Scientific economics denies that there is an observable inter-temporal ranking of purchases, but Galbraith dismisses this view as simply contrary to ordinary common sense. Historical evidence, moreover, lends further support to the hypothesis that wants tend to be ranked according to their urgency. Empirically speaking, when people are poor they tend to buy bread and simple clothing, and only later, when they are wealthy, do they buy electric tooth-brushes, automatic golf-carts and diamond jewellery. Such things must yield less satisfaction than bread since they are only later acquired: 'Presumably, the more important things come first. This ...implies a declining urgency of need.'[18] Quite simply, and using the orthodox economist's own tools of induction and observation, the fact that some things are demonstrably acquired before others may be taken as evidence that there exists an inter-temporal hierarchy of desires. All wants not being of equal standing, of course, the moral and social obligation to satisfy them is not the same.[19]

Nowadays many goods are 'of great frivolity'[20] (such as the toaster which prints an inspirational message on each piece of toast[21]), and orthodox economists are wrong to exaggerate the marginal pleasure which they yield. Galbraith recognises that it is difficult scientifically to measure changes in satisfaction over time, but, for his own part, he is convinced that 'the importance of marginal increments of all production is low and declining. The effect of increasing affluence is to minimize the importance of economic goals.'[22]

Basically, human desires are not infinite and *can* be satisfied. Witness the case of the noble savage:

The natural tendency of man, as manifested in primitive societies, is almost certainly to work until a given consumption is achieved. Then he relaxes, engages in sport, hunting, orgiastic or propitiating ceremonies or other forms of physical enjoyment or spiritual betterment. This tendency for primitive man to achieve contentment has been the despair of those who regard themselves as agents of civilization and remains so to this day. What is called economic development consists in no small part in devising strategies to overcome the tendency of men to place limits on their objectives as regards income and thus on their efforts.[23]

The positivist answer to the problem of ideology is an appeal to the evidence, and demonstrably, whatever mandarins such as Galbraith may say to the contrary, hard facts can be adduced which indicate that people are not satiated with goods and services. Demonstrably, people want more and more as society moves from rags to riches: 'Though wealth may have increased in the interim, so also may the longing for goods that must be requited. In consequence the yearning of a person for refined deodorants at a later period may be as urgent as for bread at an earlier time.'[24] Here too, however, Galbraith has an answer: such a yearning is not an authentic yearning, and is artificially implanted in the consumer by the 'well-considered mendacity'[25] of Madison Avenue, the manipulators, the hidden persuaders.

(b) Consumer preferences, Galbraith argues, are to a considerable extent not random, independent or intrinsic to the individual, but are imposed on him from outside. It is in terms of advertising and salesmanship that he chooses to explain the present-day prestige of frivolous and meaningless products that the consumer would not otherwise have demanded. In practice, the supplier in an affluent society produces not only the commodity itself but also manufactures the demand for it, and the replacement of consumer sovereignty by producer sovereignty tends to call into question the whole rationale of economic growth in the interests of want-satisfaction: 'If the individual's wants are to be urgent they must be original with himself. They cannot be urgent if they must be contrived for him. And above all they must not be contrived by the process of production by which they are satisfied. For this means that the whole case for the urgency of production, based on the urgency of wants, falls to the ground. One cannot defend production as satisfying wants if that production creates the wants.'[26]

The dependence of wants on production (what Galbraith calls the 'dependence effect' or 'revised sequence'), the recognition that production nowadays 'creates the wants it seeks to satisfy',[27] suggests that the products marginally marketed are in reality truly marginal: 'We may say that the marginal utility of present aggregate output, *ex* advertising and salesmanship, is zero.'[28] The fact that the producers of new goods are responsible for generating new wants which, in the absence of expensive and elaborate contrivance, would not have arisen spontaneously at all then raises the obvious question: 'Is a new breakfast cereal or detergent so much wanted if so much must be spent to compel in the consumer the sense of want?'[29]

Clearly, if the public is continuously being conned, empirically observed patterns of consumer behaviour cannot be taken as the index of social virtue: without a doubt, 'the revised sequence sends to the museum of obsolete ideas the notion of an equilibrium in consumer outlays which reflects the maximum of consumer satisfaction'.[30] Consumer desires may not be the result of compulsion but they do reflect sophisticated persuasion and are nonetheless artificial, created to fit in with the forward planning of the giant corporation: 'If wants are inherent they need not be contrived. But few producers of consumer goods would care to leave the purchase of their products to the spontaneous and hence unmanaged responses of the public.'[31]

What the technocrat knows, the economist does not. This latter continues to rest his case for affluence on authentic consumer needs and autonomous tastes, and to ignore the crucial role played by propaganda and want-synthesisation. Here the economist's position is analogous to that of a humanitarian 'who was long ago persuaded of the grievous shortage of hospital facilities in the town. He continues to importune the passers-by for money for more beds and refuses to notice that the town doctor is deftly knocking over pedestrians with his car to keep up the occupancy.'[32]

The secular theology and missionary zeal of the economist have the unexpected and unintended function of masking rather than revealing reality. The fact is that, in an affluent society, 'if an individual's satisfaction is less from an additional expenditure on automobiles than from one on housing, this can as well be corrected by a change in the selling strategy of General Motors as by an increased expenditure on his house'[33]; and this power to manipulate must be recognised rather than being assumed away by the misleading postulate of consumer sovereignty.[34] The GNP is revealed in its true colours as a fictive measure of welfare, since both its value and composition are the product of an endless and calculated process of illusion-creation.

Of course, not all advertising is manipulative in nature. It is traditional in trade for sellers to cry their wares, and some advertising has no purpose beyond the simple transmission of information about products on offer. One would have expected, moreover, that this function would be especially important in an affluent society offering a vast array of goods from which to choose. Galbraith, however, plays down the informative function of advertising: 'Only a gravely retarded citizen can need to be told that the American Tobacco Company has cigarettes for sale.'[35] Indeed, Galbraith argues that it is precisely because of the vast range of inessential goods and marginal services in the affluent society that the manipulative function of advertising comes into its own. Economic behaviour is only malleable and subject to management in a wealthy community: 'No hungry man who is also sober can be persuaded to use his last dollar for anything but food. But a well-fed, well-clad, well-sheltered and otherwise well-tended person can be persuaded as between an electric razor and an electric toothbrush.'[36] High-powered salesmanship, in other words, is only effective with men 'so far removed from physical want that they do not already know what they want. In this state alone men are open to persuasion.'[37] The persuader is able to guide the consumer, to sell the consumer what he wants to sell, precisely because the contemporary consumer is confused, bewildered and hasn't a clue.

Expenditure on want-creation represents a wasteful misallocation of resources, but in a world where people are overdressed and over-fed such a misallocation is no more than a trivial peccadillo: 'Our proliferation of selling activity is the counterpart of comparative affluence. Much of it is inevitable with high levels of well-being. It may be waste but it is waste that exists because the community is too well off to care.'[38] After all, want-creation only induces the consumer to buy goods which themselves represent waste of resources: 'While the forty-two million dollars worth of skill, art and paper spent in 1949 for cigarette advertising and the twenty-nine million dollars devoted to alcoholic beverages served no urgent social purpose the same is true of the cigarettes and the liquor. It is not clear that the community would be better off if those now engaged in selling tobacco and liquor were employed instead in the production of more and cheaper cigarettes and whisky.'[39]

Waste of resources is inconsequential in an affluent society. False consciousness of reality is the real problem: 'We, quite literally, advertise our commitment to immaturity, mendacity and profound gullibility. It is the hallmark of the culture. And it is justified as being economically indispensable.'[40] Nowadays, 'wants are increasingly created by the process by which they are satisfied',[41] and this means that a justification of economic growth in terms of want-satisfaction is no justification at all.

III EVALUATION

Much that Galbraith says concerning commodity-utility and manipulation cannot but strike a sympathetic note, for lurking somewhere in the soul of even the most hedonistic of readers is an ascetic Puritan suspicious of riches and luxury (and critical of the waste of resources represented by advertising and salesmanship); a Durkheimean fearful of a never-ending process of want-escalation such that the economic problem will never find a solution and the morbid psychological obsession with infinities becomes a real danger; a Marxist appalled by the tendency of vested interest via sophisticated salesmanship to attribute characteristics to commodities (such as sexual attraction or social acceptability) which are totally extrinsic to them and thereby to stimulate both collective insecurity and collective paranoia while simultaneously generating a commodity fetishism which directs attention to consuming rather than producing (and, by extension, to rights rather than to duties); a moderate convinced that men should have neither too little nor too much and anxious lest the march of events lead us progressively downhill again from the optimum reached in some previous Golden Age; an antinomian individualist unhappy to be part of a mass society regimented into an orderly queue of mass consumers waiting greedily at the gates of the Temple of Things for their turn to buy not a warm winter coat but a pair of gold-plated cuff-links. All in all, Galbraith's argument that a man buys the coat before he buys the cuff-links does have a definite plausibility, and common sense certainly does not exclude the possibility that marginal luxuries may yield less genuine or intrinsic satisfaction than do basic necessities (however difficult it would be to test this hypothesis in practice).

Of course, while it is clear that there is at least potentially an infinite quantity of consumables and while it is possible that marginal do·yield less pleasure than intra-marginal purchases, it is important to remember that a consumer's satisfactions may be regarded as additive: he does not have to forego a slice of bread and butter in order to purchase a silver-plated garlic-press, but can in an affluent society have both. The point that Galbraith is making is, however, that the cost of commodities is to be estimated not simply in terms of money but in terms of human life-forces, and that the real price of the garlic-press might turn out to be ulcers, exhaustion and thrombosis brought on by a meaningless rat-race.

In a world of affluence, an assertion that commodities are increasingly valueless and wants artificially inseminated must naturally be taken very seriously. Galbraith's views on commodity-consumption and consumer sovereignty are important and relevant, and one fully understands John Strachey's ecstatic welcome in 1958 to *The Affluent Society*:

> I have no doubt that it is a great book. It is a major work of sociology rather than economics. But in its own field it will stand being mentioned in the same breath with the one or two books which have made history in our period. . . . In fact, let me take my courage in both hands and predict that twenty years after its publication, *The Affluent Society* will be exercising an influence comparable, though of a very different kind, to that exercised by *The General Theory* today.[42]

Importance and relevance do not, however, imply accuracy in the precise statement and testing of hypotheses, and it is with the accuracy of Galbraith's model in describing the actual state of affairs in contemporary affluent societies that we shall be principally concerned in our evaluation of his views. We will group our criticisms under three headings:

(a) Persuasion and the household

In this section we will look at five criticisms of Galbraith's attitude to persuasion and the household: his neglect of latent wants, his underestimation of interdependent preference patterns, his ambiguous attitude to the problem of social change, his curious approach to the woman question and his imprecision concerning optimality and how to attain it.

Consider first the case of what Robin Marris has termed latent wants. Galbraith seems to take the fact that the desire for a particular commodity must be artificially generated as proof positive that that commodity is in some way superfluous or unnecessary. It is doubtful, however, if men really have so few genuine wants that additional desires must cynically be manufactured for them; and Galbraith's propensity to exaggerate only clouds and confuses the issue. Thus he argues that, in the revised sequence, the technostructure of the mature corporation, purely in the interests of its planned growth, decides on the frivolous gadget it wishes to market and then, via sophisticated salesmanship, instils in the consumer a taste for that trinket; and he asserts (tongue in cheek, admittedly) that 'the unopenable package, the goal of the container industry, is just around the corner'.[43] Yet Galbraith is clearly thinking of a world far more opulent than that of ordinary mortals. Perhaps the choice at the court of the Rockefellers is between 'an electric razor and an electric toothbrush'[44] (or between a fourth television set and a second automatic carving-knife), but most people face far more mundane choices. Perhaps they have been and are being induced by advertising to buy new and previously unheard-of goods such as drip-dry shirts, deodorants, washing machines, pre-packaged foods, colour televisions (since not all people like to spend the evening with a good book), but they will still nonetheless most successfully be persuaded where the new product appeals to some fundamental if possibly unexpressed need.

The point is that consumers cannot possibly themselves picture in their minds all the potential products which could satisfy the totality of their present and future needs. It is questionable, for example, if housewives recognised they had a latent need for the automatic juicer, the dishwasher or the electric mixer (or, indeed, for many other consumer durables which alleviate the burden of labour and improve the quality of work) since it is difficult effectively to 'want' something that has not yet been invented. It is less questionable, however, that housewives seized upon the new products not because of want-creation but because the hidden persuaders were only exploiting a latent desire and filling a pre-existent gap (even if one which the housewives themselves possibly had not been able clearly to formulate and articulate). Quite simply, Procter and Gamble did not invent the desire to be clean (by advertising soap and detergents) and Cadbury did not create the desire for sweetness (by marketing chocolates). As Maurice Zinkin puts it: 'If it is implied that the new want is "created" in the sense of being artificial, then this is normally not true. The new want is nearly always an old want but satisfied in a new way. . . . Can one doubt that George Washington would have flown to London for discussions if the aeroplane had existed in 1776, even though it was before the days of mass advertising?'[45] Or, as Ernest van den Haag even more explicitly argues: 'Perhaps John's desire for Mary was "contrived" by Mary who wiggled by, suggestively advertising all that she had to offer and more. Does this make his desire less genuine? Should it be frustrated simply because it has been stimulated? To be sure, if John had never seen Mary, he would not have desired her; but would he not have cared for *any* girl?'[46]

There is much to be said for tolerance in evaluating other people's latent desires, as the case of fashion illustrates. Galbraith believes that rapid change in models and styles occurs purely to serve the growth objective of the technostructure, and he asserts with apparent plausibility that the degree of producer-led change is the measure of unnecessary change. Nowadays, he argues in a characteristic passage, 'what the consumer deems to be a desirably shaped and chromatically compelling automobile is substantially different this year from what it was five years ago. But few would wish to argue that this represented a change in the consumer's intrinsic and improving vision of a vehicle – that, indeed, it was accomplished other than by rare skill, art and expense on the part of the automobile producers.'[47] Yet such an argument is misleading since, while the consumer naturally had no 'intrinsic and improving vision' of a particular vehicle, he could nonetheless have had a strong preference for change in place of stability, excitement in place of permanency, drama in place of durability; and been prepared to pay a premium for short-run fads which liven up dull lives in a way which serviceable and sensible commodities do not.

Let us turn now to a second criticism of Galbraith's attitude to persuasion and the household, namely his underestimation of the role and significance of interdependent preference patterns. Utilitarian economists have traditionally tended to postulate autonomous, random and individual ends, and it is this presumed cultural atomism which Galbraith has sought to attack by pointing to the influence on consumer choice exercised by advertising, want-manipulation and producer-power. Paradoxically, however, Galbraith has little to say about the influence on consumer choice exercised by the very process of social interaction itself, and in this respect demonstrates an unexpected lack of sociological perspective.

In practice, tastes and preferences have a high degree of social content, and it must not be forgotten that it is on *social* man that want-creating processes operate. Specifically, there are basically two cases in the sociology of consumer choice which Galbraith may justly be reproached for having neglected: prescription and emulation.

In the case of prescription, particular trinkets are widely regarded as the symbols of office habitually associated with a particular role or position in a social peer-group. Thus a stockbroker identifies himself by a bowler hat, a witch by a peaked cap, a king by a crown, and to do otherwise would be thought highly improper. The problem, as Malinowski has shown, is that once original (bodily) needs are satisfied, and as a result of the process of satisfying them, new and secondary needs develop which are imposed on the individual by the group and which severely limit his freedom of choice. No amount of sophisticated salesmanship could persuade a banker living in London to conform to the norms of dress and shelter that would be regarded as eminently suitable by a Trobriand Islander, and in ignoring such culturally induced group tastes and the pressure exerted by all upon each when men live together in communities, Galbraith shows excessive individualism in his approach and reveals his vestigal utilitarianism.

In the case of emulation, particular goods (usually those of considerable expense) are purchased once again in a social context rather than a social vacuum, and are associated with an attempt to impress, keep up with, even overtake the Joneses next door. Emulation is the key force in Thorstein Veblen's theory of 'conspicuous consumption', and also in James Duesenberry's 'relative income hypothesis' (according to which when income rises consumption is expected to rise but when income falls consumption is not expected to fall, this 'ratchet effect' being due to an acquired awareness that one consumes under the watchful eyes of neighbours, colleagues and friends), and it is not entirely absent from Galbraith's own work. Galbraith appears to feel, however, that emulation is principally a force to be reckoned with in so far as it is engendered by and channelled through the calculated sales-effort of professionals and experts. Such an attitude grossly underestimates the autonomous momentum inherent in social phenomena themselves. It is odd that, while having so little to say about spontaneous emulation in a stratified society, Galbraith still acknowledges its importance for a stratified world: 'When hunger is appeased, savings will not increase if another and higher living standard is known to people and is accepted by them as a norm. The whole world lives under the "demonstration effect" of American living standards; American amenities and gadgets have become the goal of people the world around.'[48] It is likely that a similar 'demonstration effect' operates within affluent societies, and that Galbraith for this reason ought to have provided a more complete analysis of the position of goods and services within the matrix of social relationships. After all, the fact that advertising is able to exploit the correlation between inequality of wealth and inequality of commodity-utility does not mean that it is responsible for that correlation, or that even in the absence of planned persuasion the relatively deprived would not envy the relatively privileged their elegant status-symbols and seek to earn money (by producing goods and services and thereby generating that very economic growth which Galbraith argues is the product of producer-power) in order to purchase those symbolic luxuries. The Afghan hound, for instance, is both a status-symbol and a source of great happiness in itself; and the fact that the hound is unadvertised has not prevented its charms from becoming widely known and its consumption widely emulated. The choice here, in short, is not between atomism and promotion (as Galbraith would have us believe) but rather between atomism and social interaction.

Our third criticism of Professor Galbraith's views on persuasion and the household concerns the problem of social change in a world of affluence, a problem which exists because of a possible contradiction in Galbraith's model: on the one hand he regards excessive ambition, the multiplication of wants and the pursuit of luxury as unhealthy, but on the other hand he is anything but traditionalist and conservative in his social attitudes. Yet it is likely that to retard or arrest changes in demand (both quantitative and qualitative, i.e. both in terms of more goods and of different goods) would be to repress innovation, challenge and novelty; and that some economic growth and some insecurity are the price that must be paid for institutional reform. The ever-present threat in Galbraith's work that the emancipation of belief might lead to the ossification of the *status quo* into a quasi-Weberian 'traditional standard of living' suggests that to some observers the model could well appear reactionary rather than radical.

Moralists and ascetics have long challenged the supremacy of material values and the inordinate estimation of wealth; and in the case of Galbraith it is difficult not to suspect that this challenge, together with the implicit puritanism one detects in so much of his work, may be traced back to the 'uncompromising Calvinism'[49] of his childhood in Iona Station, Ontario, where as elsewhere hard work and minimal luxury were characteristic of the Protestant Ethic. The Scotch (as they called themselves) had a remarkable respect for money and spent it reluctantly (and then not on luxuries): 'This was, I think, pure love. Some have always wanted money for what it would buy. Some have wanted it for the power it conferred. Some have sought it for the prestige it provided. The Scotch wanted it for its own sake. . . . Two techniques for accumulating assets have always been in some measure in competition. One is to earn money; the other is to avoid spending it. Our neighbours enthusiastically employed both.'[50] Possibly because of a childhood spent (like Veblen) in a world both agrarian and puritanical, Galbraith has a definite propensity to regard rapid and continual change in the direction of commodity-affluence as the stormy petrel of national decadence. What he neglects, however, is that stagnation and stalemate may be even more unhealthy for a people.

The fourth criticism of Galbraith's attitude to persuasion and the household refers to his curious attitude to the woman question. To begin with, his assertions are misleading since he fails to stress that approaching half of American women now hold jobs outside the home: on the evidence, it appears not to be the case that the need to administer consumption converts women into a crypto-servant class, but rather that labour-saving consumer durables (replacing paid home-helps) actually make it possible for wives to go out to work. Then, too, he forgets that, because it is often the wife's income that permits marginal families to enjoy an affluent standard of living, such work is a definite source of liberation in so far as it causes many husbands to deliberate together with their wives on matters such as the family budget or the place of residence. He has, moreover, a strangely ambivalent attitude to work and leisure. He recognises that painting can be a source of satisfaction but does not appear to regard cooking, sewing and decorating in the same light.

He tends to accept that the housewife denied professional fulfill-ment will become bored, frustrated, alcoholic, even neurotic, but tends also to neglect the potential neuroses that may be engendered in small children if consigned to a succession of paid nurses. Nor does he recommend that the problem of maternal deprivation be attacked by paternal substitution, where the father stays at home and becomes a houseperson in place of his spouse. Galbraith's emphasis on finding ways to release the woman while not ensnaring the man shows a surprising acceptance of the work-ethic.

Naturally many women do obtain job-satisfaction from work outside the home (women such as the middle-class graduate housewives of and for whom Galbraith is clearly writing). Yet if such women work, then something is bound to be produced; and that which is produced must be consumed. Here the implication seems to be that consumption (even consumption dependent on artificially inseminated wants) should be regarded as the veil of tears through which all must pass in order that some can enter the paradise of production. On the other hand, however, many women do not obtain job-satisfaction from work outside the home, but seek employment only so as to permit their families the luxury of purchases which Galbraith would dismiss as frivolous and useless. It is not easy to see why the women who fall into this latter category should be freed from the drudgery of the home only to discover the drudgery of the office or the production-line instead.

The fifth and last criticism of Galbraith's attitude to persuasion and the household focuses on his imprecision concerning optimality and how to attain it. Here the dilemma is that, while Galbraith clearly believes there exists a threshold beyond which goods lose their urgency, he neglects to say at what precise level of prosperity an individual or a society may be regarded as having enough. Basic needs for food can, after all, be satisfied by uncooked meat, for housing by a cave, for clothing by animal skins; and once mankind passes beyond this physical minimum it enters into a range of uncertainty in which it requires more guidance from the economic philosopher than is forthcoming in Galbraith's work. Galbraith's imprecision as to the correct measures of poverty and wealth (he never says whether America as a nation is actually economically overweight, or whether it is not simply the case that some 'fat cats' are getting more than they need), his reluctance to indicate what he regards as the ideal quantity and composition of consumption (he never says that the three-car family ought to be a one-car family or specifies how many hats a well-dressed woman may with propriety purchase), leave his model excessively vague; and this is a particular source of disappointment to the sympathetic reader who suspects that there may be some truth in Galbraith's assertion that too much is very definitely too much. Galbraith accepts that the need for economic growth is still urgent in developing countries; it is a pity that he does not also suggest some criterion by which they can know when they are fully developed so as to avoid the disaster of overdevelopment which, he appears to believe, is the impending tragedy of contemporary America.

If Americans are potentially overdressed, overfed, overhoused, overheated and (as the price for all the former) overworked, and if the basic cause of these excesses is salesmanship and persuasion, then there would appear to be a case for controls. Galbraith, however, omits to propose such controls, and is content to leave the problem of manipulation elucidated but in essence unresolved. He is opposed to discriminatory taxation of advertising and promotion, and he does not recommend an extension of countervailing power in the form of State-sponsored consumer protection services aimed at breaking the link between information and propaganda by supplying impartial, accurate and dependable intelligence. He praises private watchdogs such as Ralph Nader but does not make an expansion of their activities (reinforced by adequate financial assistance from the community) an important part of his policy-programme. His basic message is a call for general education and a plea for consumers to become aware of demand-engineering and attempt to resist it; but such a message is an invitation to pessimism. It represents, after all, continual frustration (since the household must at all times be trying to guess whether a particular advertisement is informative or manipulative in nature) and frequent failure (since when one hardly knows whom to believe one is bound to make mistakes); it means that the financial burden of information costs is often transferred back to the household (as where the potential buyer must himself pay a fee to acquire reliable advice); and it leaves unsolved the problem of waste (for even if Galbraith is right in his contention that advertising is no more a misallocation of resources than are many of the goods it publicises, he is surely wrong to underestimate the significance of such misallocation in a world where the alternative to work remains leisure and the alternative to private provision remains better school meals and higher State pensions for the elderly).

On a practical level, the furthest Galbraith is willing to go is to recommend a non-commercial alternative to commercial television,[51] making the implicit assertion that there is no hidden persuasion in organisations such as the BBC and that their technostructure is socially accountable in practice as well as in theory. Yet, even while accepting that independence of the media from both commercial and political influences is an important objective, it would be wrong to underestimate the complexity of the problem. The media in the private sector are financially dependent on advertising revenues, which end up paying for programmes and publications in many cases of high quality; while the advertising industry itself provides work for artists and writers whose output is not always entirely without aesthetic or entertainment value. Were the media to become totally non-commerical, moreover, as would be the case were all advertising to be banned, then the consumer would have to pay the economic cost for his television viewing and his newspapers, just as he already pays the economic cost for his books and his films; and this in turn might mean repression of pluralism (as where a higher price leads to a smaller quantity demanded and possibly thereby reduces the range of alternatives that are commercially viable). Of course, the consumer would not have to pay the economic cost of the media if they were to be run as social services and in receipt of a grant from the Exchequer (on behalf of the general taxpayer); but such a solution would be expensive, open to the threat of political pressure and sophisticated censorship, and lacking in the sensitivity that results from the ability to relate a *specific* cost to a *specific* benefit.

In any case, Galbraith does not propose that the media become totally non-commercial. He only proposes that a non-commercial alternative to commercial television be provided. His solution is as unsatisfying as his diagnosis is grave.

(b) Persuasion and the producer

Turning now from the relationship between persuasion and demand to that between persuasion and supply, we shall examine in this section three topics conspicuous by their absence from Galbraith's theory of producer-power: the failure of want-creation, the cost of manipulation and the problem of competitive retaliation.

First, the failure of want-creation. Galbraith argues that the customer, nowadays no longer subject to the tyranny of hunger and the elements, has tastes 'in some measure malleable'[52] which the corporation can, 'to the best of its ability',[53] subordinate to the goals of its planning; but the inclusion of one *caveat* after another is a hint from Galbraith himself that pliability is not infinite, so that the firm may fail as well as succeed in its attempt to bend the consumer to its will. Galbraith gives the example of the Edsel ('a very large vehicle with something of the physiognomy of a surprised frog'[54]) as a case in point where a firm made losses because it incorrectly judged the demands (real and potential) of consumers; and this suggests (unless it is to be regarded as a freak occurrence meriting no more than a footnote) that the mature corporation is not always able to sell a planned X units of good Y at price Z because of its alleged ability to tailor the market to its requirements. A hypothesis not simply of 'producer power' but of 'producer sovereignty' is an exaggeration at the best of times; and it appears, moreover, totally inapplicable to the vast numbers of sales made directly by one firm to another (since experts are clearly more likely to be interested in price, quantity and quality than in product image).

Producers naturally try to create wants. Whether or not they succeed, however, is quite a different matter; and the cause of scientific accuracy is not served by Galbraith's tendency to underplay the constraints that limit the power of planners and to underestimate the frequency of failures. Galbraith exaggerates the extent to which the businessman always hits on exactly the right product and markets it with precisely the right appeal to the consumer, and in so doing is providing a spurious rationalisation of conduct both to buyer (who is pleased to blame his obesity and promiscuity on Them rather than Us) and to seller (who is reluctant to admit that he still lives in a world of uncertainty where the future is determined as much by guesstimate as by plan). Such an exaggerated account of the effectiveness of persuasion (reflecting no doubt the view of Madison Avenue itself concerning the extent to which it is indispensable to the modern capitalist economy) also serves to conceal deeper cultural problems. The fact that people are susceptible to advertisements for alcohol and cigarettes, for instance, might in the last analysis be a symptom of ingrained social stress, anxiety and dissatisfaction for which society and not advertising must take the blame.

Not only does Galbraith's model not incorporate the problem of failure, but it is incapable of doing so. The model does not explain what would happen to corporate planning should consumers discover that meaningless trinkets do not in fact bring the promised happiness or prestige (possibly because in a society characterised by mass production, advertising-induced emulation is to some extent an exercise in mutual frustration). Should consumers recognise the existence of persuasion and contract out of control, then the whole planning system (and thus the economy) would be destabilised. Galbraith seems unaware of the irony that books such as his own, by making the consumer aware of manipulation, represent a considerable threat to the modern capitalist economy as he perceives it to be.

An assumption of success rather than failure of bamboozlement might mean the exploitation of the consumer in the form of higher prices and lesser output than would have obtained in a more competitive environment. Galbraith, of course, is adamant that corporate growth and moderate prices habitually go together: 'The prices that are so set – that reflect the affirmative purposes of the technostructure – will almost always be lower, and on occasion much lower, than those that would maximise profits over some period relevant to managerial calculation.'[55] Yet Galbraith is here associating the objective of sales-maximisation with the pre-existence of a stable price-sensitive downward-sloping demand curve, whereas his own stress on the efficacy of salesmanship would lead one to expect instead a shift outwards in the demand curve. In such a way advertising might take the place of price-reduction as a means of attracting customers and sales-maximisation might become tragically compatible with profit-maximisation.

Second, the cost of manipulation. As Professor Gordon puts it: 'If the management of demand costs anything, an efficient technostructure would try to accommodate whatever independent preferences consumers possess rather than try to mold them into exotic shapes'.[56] The increasing cost of trying to persuade marginal consumers to buy marginal units of marginal trinkets might in short cause the producer to concentrate instead on those goods which the consumer is known to want. The constraint on producer sovereignty imposed by the well-known fact that even duplicity has its price is nonetheless grossly understated in Galbraith's model.

In fairness to Galbraith, however, two comments ought to be made. Firstly, Galbraith in his reply to Gordon has admitted the relevance of the cost argument and accepted that technocrats are prepared to follow the consumer as well as to lead him.[57] Then, secondly, Galbraith's very definition of 'planning' includes market research alongside advertising and salesmanship, suggesting once again that not even in the Galbraithian world can just anything be sold at just any price.

Consumer preferences are certainly far easier to predict than to synthesise, but even prediction itself often fails because of the complex and nebulous mix of qualities the consumer looks for in a product: price, quantity and image certainly, but also taste, smell, feel, colour, shape. Many technically excellent products fail to find a market, moreover, because of the lag between the time when the need is identified and the time when the commodity is offered for sale; for in the interim, while research and development was being conducted and new plant installed, tastes, fancies and whims might capriciously have altered. All in all, and despite the views of Professor Galbraith, business activity remains inseparable from risk.

Market research may be seen as no more than an attempt to forecast (in order to satisfy) the future desires of sovereign consumers. Galbraith, however, prefers to see it in a sinister light, as an attempt to ensnare the sovereign by discovering not so much what he will want as what he can be made to want. Here he is being excessively dramatic; for exposition is not the same as propaganda nor investigation the same as control.

Third, the problem of competitive retaliation. Galbraith believes, as we have seen, that in modern industrial environments each oligopolist in practice ends up with 'a reasonably reliable share of the market',[58] and is convinced that large-scale advertising is in no way an attempt to elbow one's competitor out of his traditional seat. This assumption of complete market segmentation (with its implication that each producer has an unchallenged and unchallengeable position) is, however, an unrealistic one, as G. C. Allen has pointed out:

> Oligopolists may for a time keep out of one another's way, may respect one another's markets and may refrain from direct price competition. But if they are producing at different levels of cost, as they often are, this situation is unstable. The firms that make the highest profits will be able to finance investments in improved products or processes and will in the end be able to move into their laggard rivals' markets. If their main purpose is expansion, as Galbraith supposes, they will hardly neglect such an opportunity.[59]

There is no reason to assume (as Galbraith does) that rival corporations within an industry attempt via advertising and salesmanship simply to attract new customers to a particular product, while simultaneously still refusing to direct their aggressive competitiveness against one another. Were this hypothesis to be accurate (and it is one of the few testable hypotheses to be found in Galbraith's work), then one would expect a secular shift in demand away from product A (which is not advertised) and towards product B (which is). Wilder, however, who tested the hypothesis empirically using American data on advertising and 27 consumer goods industries in the period 1948–1967, returned a negative verdict: 'The hypothesis that advertising affects the distribution of spending among industries finds little support from these results.'[60] Indeed, his findings seem to suggest that households decide independently on the amount of their income they wish to allocate to a particular commodity, leaving advertising with an unexpectedly residual intra-industry function: 'If advertising is effective, its major effect is to alter market shares within an industry rather than to increase the general demand for the product'.[61]

Such a result makes sense in the light of historical evidence, which confirms that corporations have slipped back or leapt ahead in the league table of profitability and size and demonstrates that giants in the past have not always succeeded in immunising themselves against changes in market shares. It also illustrates how a clear contradiction between the corporate goals of security and growth may emerge; for my growth will cost your security should I develop more rapidly than the market for the product as a whole and hence feel compelled to invade your territory and steal your customers (just as in the Galbraithian model a rapidly developing car industry presumably seeks to reallocate the national expenditure away from the sleepy toaster industry and thus rob it of security).

In a world of competition between brands for shares in a given or a growing total, my advertising competes with your advertising and converts your plan from a forecast to a target that may not in fact be attained. I am, moreover, uncertain about your reaction to my sales strategy and must build your probable policies into my own plan. And I am fearful lest an arms-race situation develop such that my large-scale advertising in practice only serves to cancel out the effects of your large-scale advertising. The likelihood of such a stand-off, however, Galbraith regards as minimal, arguing (as we have indicated) that in the event of wasteful mutual neutralisation 'steps would long ago have been taken to limit advertising outlays by common agreement'.[62]

Such an argument is unsatisfactory. It appears to contradict the more fundamental Galbraithian hypothesis that brands do not compete with brands but products with products; refers to no actual historical instances where the effect was in operation; and pre-supposes a degree of overt collusion that is in most countries illegal. It applies, moreover, exclusively to the highly specialised uni-product giant, and not to the conglomerate which, by spreading itself thin over a number of markets rather than dominating one alone, is bound as a result to be a more vulnerable price-taker than the absolute size of its corporate parent would suggest.

In practice, most markets are far more competitive than Galbraith believes them to be; and, since no corporation can plan for its competitors, it is likely that producers will concentrate on those goods which are likely most quickly and easily to find customers. Producer-power should not be overstated: industries can and do develop without significant reliance on persuasion (witness the phenomenal success of the computer industry), others can and do decline despite the powers of persuasion at their disposal (the fate of cinemas), while should new desires be mainly the product of manipulation new products would be principally those best suited to the production-runs of giant corporations (and this has not necessarily been the case, as with small fashion boutiques which have sprung up to service a whole new set of consumer preferences). Even in the affluent society, it is doubtful if the consumer really allows himself to be led by the nose by the Colgate ring of confidence.

(c) Persuasion and social balance

Material goods and aesthetic or cultural objectives are not mutually exclusive. The car gives greater freedom to tour in scenic and historic regions or to dwell outside the city centre; television can broadcast documentaries, first-class plays and even serve as an Open University to raise the educational level of those citizens unable to attend a full-time institution; the yacht, the ski-lift, the hi-fi, the jet, are all valuable complements to leisure.

Moreover, since socially provided benefits and facilities cost money, economic growth is the prime source (at least in the absence of a general sharing-out of existing wealth) of new resources necessary for increased State activity. Talking admittedly of poor countries, Galbraith himself recognises this fact: 'Only as increased production income is available does good education become possible. Only from this will there be wherewithal to support schools and colleges and universities. Economic growth is necessary if a nation is to pay for schools and teachers'.[63] Whereas in a static economy if the social sector is to expand tax rates will have to be put up, in a growing economy both social and private sectors can grow together, since a rising national income means an expanding mass of taxation even with rates kept constant and thus an increasing pool of resources at the disposal of the government to be used to correct deficiencies in the social fabric. This pool of resources arises without a specific redistributive shift from one sector to the other; and the fact that rates remain constant despite a major governmental campaign to equalise opportunity also means that reallocation of life-chances can occur without any need for redistribution of current income. Economic growth can thus generate improved social welfare for some without necessitating diminished economic welfare for others. It is the ultimate antidote to the zero-sum game. Politically speaking, moreover, it is easier to bring about change of any sort in an evolving situation than in a static one, where changes in the balance of power are as a result often explosive and revolutionary rather than marginal and gradual.

Economic growth, however, implies the development of new commodities, and the demand for these commodities Galbraith tends to dismiss as engineered and artificial. We seem, in other words, to be confronted with a choice between social reform and balance on the one hand, and authenticity and spontaneity of desires on the other. The choice is a fictitious one; for Galbraith in the last analysis is hardly a romantic looking backwards towards some mythical state of nature where men were able to be themselves and desires were innate, as Anthony Crosland assumed him to be. In fact, both Galbraith and Crosland adopted a very similar attitude to wants artificially created, namely that the observer should withhold judgement until he knows the nature of the wants and the motives of the manipulators. As Crosland put it: 'In most countries a large proportion of the population feels little want for education, and the want has to be not merely stimulated but actually enforced by compulsory state education: are we then to say that the provision of education is not urgent? The spontaneous demand for typhoid or diphtheria immunisation is manifestly weak and must be fortified by government publicity campaigns: is it therefore to be brushed aside as inessential?'[64] Yet, quite simply, Galbraith does not brush it aside, and this reminds us of the fundamental double asymmetry of his model.

First, Galbraith believes that almost all the preferences in an affluent society are induced by élites; and that want-creation by a socially conscious political and intellectual meritocracy (on behalf of schools, hospitals, roads and theatres) is at least more tolerable than want-creation by the narrow and selfish men of the technostructure (on behalf of electric toothbrushes and private motor-cars). Thus, while Galbraith on the one hand attacks the blandishments of private advertising and salesmanship, he on the other hand clearly sees himself as a crusader carrying on an unrelenting campaign of political and social propaganda on behalf of the kind of future society he personally most favours. His disparagement of aggregates and growth rates hence turns out to be a red herring, for Galbraith in the last analysis is more critical of *what* is produced and consumed than of production and consumption *per se*. His fundamental distinction is clearly not between original and acquired wants at all, but rather between wants which he regards as moral and wants which he regards as contrary to the public purpose.[65]

Second, Galbraith believes that true democracy is political even if not economic; and affirms strongly that the individual can be counted on to vote intelligently for progressive politicians who will spend his money wisely on his behalf. The failure of economic democracy, however, hardly augurs well for the future of political democracy; for if the ignorant and bamboozled masses are unable to resist the contrivances of commercial advertising, how then will they cope with the product-image of politicians and parties, let alone digest the intellectually demanding arguments of party-political broadcasts? Fleet Street and Smith Square can be as manipulative as Madison Avenue; and in view of Galbraith's healthy respect for the powers of persuasion there is no reason to suppose that the electorate can be counted upon dependably to vote for courageous radicals rather than lapdog reactionaries – if the packaging is right.

6 The Political Market

Galbraith recommends greater governmental intervention in the production, distribution and exchange of goods and services. He also recommends, however, that if power to decide is to be redistributed from individuals and firms *towards* the State, then the power to decide must first be redistributed *within* the State and specifically away from bureaucrats and in favour of politicians.

In this chapter we will examine, first, why the bureaucrat is not a friend to the public interest; second, in what circumstances the politician will dependably maximise social well-being; and, third, what Galbraith identifies as the proper scope for governmental direction and control on behalf of the community as a whole. In conclusion we shall suggest some criticisms of Galbraith's theory of the political market.

I THE CASE AGAINST THE BUREAUCRAT

Galbraith believes that there exists a dual imbalance in present-day intervention: namely an imbalance between sectors (support tends to go to the powerful planning system rather than to the weak market system or the social welfare complex) and an imbalance between projects (aid is heavily biased in favour of defence and defence-related industries). The cause of this imbalance (together with the associated ideology and imagery) is to be sought in the interaction between bureaucracies, public and private, and in particular in the Scylla of symbiosis and the Charybdis of inertia:

(a) 'Bureaucratic symbiosis' (the organic interdependence of technocracy and civil service) has developed to such an extent that the line between huge corporation and machinery of State has become 'increasingly artificial and indistinct'[1]: 'The modern state . . . is not the executive committee of the bourgeoisie, but it *is* more nearly the executive committee of the technostructure.'[2] For such intimacy three reasons may be advanced.

First, there is complementarity of interest. The public bureaucracy resembles the corporate technostructure in so far as both organisations 'are served by growth and the consequent promotions, pay, perquisites, prestige and power'[3]; and since often the expansion of one bureaucracy leads to a welcome expansion in the other (the growth of the Atomic Energy Commission, for example, resulting from a grant given to a supplying industry to develop new atomic weaponry), public and private organisations have a tendency to find and pursue common purposes. Structure clearly relates effectively to structure: 'Rarely does the private technostructure meet a public bureaucracy without discovering some area in which there can be co-operation to mutual advantage.'[4]

The power to influence government policy is hence not spread evenly throughout the economy; for the power of producers in some sectors is very great (say, of the giant firm in the electronics industry, where bureaucratic symbiosis obtains) while in others it is insignificant (say, of the small shop-keeper or of the small businessman in a service industry, whose only contact with the State is his elected but ineffectual Parliamentarian). Of course, some parts of the market system do successfully influence public policy through visible pressure on legislators (this is the case, for instance, with American farmers). Most, however, have little or no influence precisely because they cannot operate effectively on or through the public bureaucracy:

> As the individual member of the market system cannot typically influence his customers, so he cannot influence the state. The president of General Motors has a prescriptive right, on visiting Washington, to see the President of the United States. The president of General Electric has a right to see the Secretary of Defense and the president of General Dynamics to see any general. The individual farmer has no similar access to the Secretary of Agriculture; the individual retailer has no entrée to the Secretary of Commerce. It would be of little value to them if they did. The public bureaucracy . . . can be effectively and durably influenced only by another organization.[5]

One hand washes the other; hands unable to wash are unlikely to be washed.

Second, there is regular interchange of personnel, as is revealed by the following information relating to the military-industrial complex:

> In February, 1969, 2,072 former officers of the rank of Navy captain, Army colonel or better were working for defense contractors, and a very large number of these – 210 at Lockheed, 141 at McDonnell-Douglas, 113 at General Dynamics, 104 at North American Rockwell – were with the specialized defense contractors. Meanwhile, men from the industry (of whom the most notable in the present Administration is the former chairman of the Hewlett-Packard Company, David Packard, the Deputy Secretary of Defense) go to Washington to man that end of the combined operation.[6]

This common market in personnel may be taken as an important reason for the large share of government spending that goes on defence, and also for the apparent willingness of Pentagon bureaucrats (possibly looking forward to a future green pasture somewhere in the munitions field) to become 'commercial accessories of General Dynamics'.[7]

Interchange of executive talent exists in other areas besides armaments (between, for example, the Department of Transportation and General Motors); and it is no surprise to find that corporations in these areas too tend to benefit from governmental largesse unrelated to wider considerations of genuine social need.

Third, there is the 'Principle of Consistency', which specifies that the goals of individual, organisation and society will be consistent and gives some hints on causality: 'The goals of the mature corporation will be a reflection of the goals of the members of the technostructure. And the goals of the society will tend to be those of the corporation.'[8]

Galbraith is convinced that the evidence lends support to his hypothesis that nowadays the goals of the technostructure (job-satisfaction, security and growth) have become those of the nation (witness the high social valuation of technological innovation, professional expertise and rising standards of living).[9] He adds, however, that although social attitudes are to a considerable extent derived from the needs of the technostructure, those attitudes are nonetheless assumed, by the technocracy as well as by the general public, to have 'original social purpose'[10]; and this distancing effect in turn gives the technocrat the warm feeling of serving the social interest when he is in fact only conforming to a discipline which he has himself imposed on the community.[11] His problem appears to be not so much premeditated malice as acute absence of mind, but this cost has its benefit, since the organisation man is able in this way to convince himself that he is socially useful: 'The individual member of the technostructure identifies himself with the goals of the mature corporation as, and because, the corporation identifies itself with goals which have, or appear to him to have, social purpose.'[12] Since State bureaucrat as well as corporate technocrat likes to feel he is serving rather than dominating his society, the two men ultimately find themselves symbiotically united via the plastic umbilical cord of a manipulated social consensus, and are able to convince themselves and each other that their work is motivated less by love of a pay-cheque than by loyalty and service to the collective consciousness.

A good illustration of symbiosis through deference to a presumed social objective is the defence of the Fatherland. Munitions firms have a vested interest in an aggressive foreign policy (although, as Galbraith puts it, 'there is something uniquely obscene about competition to promote weapons of mass destruction for purposes of improving the stock-market position of a corporation'[13] and attempt to interest decision-makers in new weapons systems able to carry out new missions which require such instruments, while the army has a specific need 'for the occupation, prestige, promotions that go with active military operations' and the Air Force 'for bombing as a *raison d'être*'[14]; but neither the defence contractors nor the military can be accused of seeking expansion purely in the service of organisational self-interest. Rather, both groups of organisation men have internalised the widespread social belief in the existence of the Communist threat and the permanence of the Cold War. Galbraith knows that 'what is done and what is believed are, first and naturally, what serve the goals of the bureaucracy itself'.[15] Organisation men do not benefit from this knowledge; and end up in consequence the victims of their own propaganda, overjoyed to be serving social goals which they have themselves unknowingly but unambiguously manufactured. And because organisation men in both the planning system and the machinery of State share a common perception of the public interest, they constitute a monolithic alliance able to exert excessive influence on citizen and politician and thus to ensure that their common needs and purposes will be furthered.

(b) 'Bureaucratic inertia' (the organisational momentum and resistance to change that is a powerful force in perpetuating existing institutions and beliefs even when conditions have altered and made those institutions and beliefs obsolete) accounts for much of the inflexibility and conservatism of highly organised structures: 'Bureaucracy can always continue to do what it is doing. It is incapable, on its own, of a drastic change of course.'[16] Bureaucrats tend to have a picture of reality that is almost by definition inaccurate and out of date, and the reasons are as follows:

First, bureaucratic structures tend to advance the rubber man who substitutes obsequiousness to superiors for firmness of character and who has studiously avoided controversy[17]; for a bureaucracy is above all 'governed not by the truth but by its own truth. It defends its truth against the reality. Those who question its truth are discounted for eccentricity, ignored for ineffectiveness or excluded for unreliability.'[18] Galbraith himself discovered, as American Ambassador to India from 1961 to 1963, that acceptance of the approved belief means participation, while non-conformity means exclusion: 'If . . . you insist on the uncomplicated truth, you are not effective but a problem to be handled. You do not participate; you are told afterwards.'[19] Some, indeed, who have, within the State Department, the audacity to challenge the 'over-age and weary ideas and the over-used and tired men on which our foreign policy, as it is known, depends',[20] are likely to be rewarded for their alienation from the conventional wisdom not by being promoted but by being 'selected out'.[21]

Second, bureaucracies tend to suffer from isolation, resentment of outsiders and an obsession with autonomy: 'The tendency – the inevitable tendency – of any large organization, public or private, is to be authoritarian and exclusive. It pursues its purposes and minimizes outside interference, and does so not because it is wicked but because that is the nature of organization.'[22]

The love of autonomy leads to caution and an excessive fear of controversy: 'The modern foreign-policy expert is a man who knows what should be done but has exceptionally sophisticated reasons for not wishing to risk criticism.'[23] For, just as the technostructure of the mature corporation fears interference from the ignorant share-holder, so quite a few civil servants regard legislators as, 'second only to the Communists, the prime enemy of American foreign policy'[24] and consequently avoid decisions which would arouse contest in the political arena by falling back on the twin techniques of 'piously reasoned inaction'[25] ('We could better defend our policy if the Department would get off its ass on various matters and provide one'[26]) and appeal to tradition[27] ('One feature of the State Department mind on which I find I have not mellowed is its profound moral conviction that established policy is to be preferred to the one that is best for the United States'[28]). Most conferences in the State Department are consequently 'not devoted to assessing the wisdom of a particular policy. They are concerned with what will be said on Capitol Hill.'[29] Fortunately for the bureaucrat, however, the threat of political interference is minimal: because of the multiplicity of operations and policies and the 'revolving-door nature of higher Washington officialdom', the fact is that 'few men in the executive branch remain in office long enough to have knowledge of the affairs of which, nominally, they are in charge',[30] while few men in the legislative branch are ever adequately consulted.

Tangential organisations such as the CIA are particularly free from scrutiny: 'An overseas bureaucracy, once in existence, develops a life and purpose of its own. Control by Washington is exiguous. Control by the Congress is for practical purposes non-existent.'[31] Such organisations have a vested interest in secrecy (for spies and agents organised in bureaucratic structures are fully aware that their funding would be jeopardised were their high failure-rate and low cost-effectiveness to become known[32] and are not noticeably receptive to new ideas.

Third, bureaucracies tend to experience elephantiasis so acute that it is 'capable of slowing all progress to a walk or less'[33]; and size not only means delays and postponements while agreement is being sought (since 'every civilized group acts in some degree by unanimous consent'[34]) but also built-in continuity of policy and adherence to precedent as a means of securing consensus (since 'one cannot get agreement on anything new. When a deadline approaches everyone repairs hurriedly to what was agreed several years ago'[35]). In the case of foreign policy, it is in substantial measure the sheer size of the State Department which 'freezes it to all of its antique positions'[36] and ensures the perpetuation of the *status quo*: 'Nothing in my view is so important as to get the Department back to manageable size.'[37]

A good illustration of inertia rationalised in terms of bureaucratic truth is the American superpower mystique, which turns out to be based 'on official convenience and belief . . . rather than on the underlying reality'[38] and to have been articulated by 'people who formed their ideas in the 1940s and 1950s and have never changed them as the world has changed.'[39] Policy based on established stereotypes and accustomed ways of thinking is, however, dangerous policy, for it can lead to spectacularly inappropriate action. The abortive landing of American-sponsored anti-Castro forces at the Bay of Pigs in Cuba in 1961, for instance, is 'a textbook case of bureaucratic self-deception': 'Organization needed to believe that Fidel Castro was toppling on the edge. Communism was an international conspiracy; hence it could have no popular local roots; hence the Cuban people would welcome the efforts to overthrow it. Intelligence was made to confirm these beliefs. If it didn't it was, by definition, defective information.'[40] Yet whereas bureaucratic truth 'held that Communists being visibly wicked and having no indigenous support, Castro could easily be ousted', real truth reveals 'that he had wide support',[41] as the invading forces rapidly discovered to their cost. Again, another mistake that might have been avoided had second-rate men not been taken in by the parroting of perverted perceptions was American involvement in Vietnam. Bureaucratic truth, heavily committed to the image of 'a planet threatened by an imminent takeover by the unified and masterful forces of the Communist world'[42] and unable to encompass the realities of the situation (which it treated as 'uninformed, perverse and very wrong'[43]), sealed its proponents ever more hermetically into the ideological cocoon which they had spun for themselves and made them genuinely convinced that their habitual view of things accurately described external reality: 'What was essentially a civil war between the Vietnamese was converted into an international conflict with rich ideological portent for all mankind. South Vietnamese dictators became incipient Jeffersonians holding aloft the banners of an Asian democracy. Wholesale graft became an indispensable aspect of free institutions.'[44] The inevitable result was 'disaster magnified by postponement'[45] and ought to serve as a warning to the future against the misleading and biased advice of bureaucrats in the Pentagon and State Department of today, whose organisational interest ('The ABM, the new generation manned bomber and the nuclear aircraft carriers serve not the balance of terror, but the organizations that build and operate them'[46]) and outdated ideology ('Troop levels and deployment in Europe are still tied to the panic fears of twenty years ago when a march westwards by the Red Army seemed imminent') cause them to oppose moves towards peaceful coexistence and deceleration of the arms race for reasons more compatible with bureaucratic than with national purpose.

Bureaucratic symbiosis and bureaucratic inertia are to Galbraith the key explanatory variables in unravelling the present-day imbalance in governmental intervention in the economy. The point, however, as Galbraith so disarmingly implies, is to change it.

II THE CASE FOR THE POLITICIAN

Technocrats and bureaucrats have their own goals and beliefs; and at present, mainly because two monoliths shout loudly when they shout in unison, 'the fox is powerful in the management of the coop'.[47] Radical politicians, however, are the guardians of the public interest, and must consequently set themselves the task of 'the recapture of power from organization'.[48] Accompanying their conquest of the commanding heights should be five reforms in the basic fabric of the American political system itself:

(i) If power is to be exercised in the public interest, then it must be exercised principally by the legislative branch of government. This is a surprising recommendation, for legislators are selected by small electorates in constituencies where a large firm or key industry may predominate (whereas the President is elected by all the individuals, regions and groupings that make up the nation as a whole) and may also be more open to influence from outside lobbies than is the executive (which as a result appears to emerge the better custodian of the national interest). Galbraith believes, however, that legislators are able to emancipate themselves from the power of the organisation man; and argues that there is probably less bribery than was once the case, that strong corporate lobbies are challenged by the countervailing power of environmental and consumerist lobbies and that the modern corporation man is less likely than was the old-style owner-entrepreneur to meet politicians too frequently on a social basis (partly because the modern technocrat is more a function that a face, partly because modern business is increasingly national and international rather than constituency-based).

The executive, regrettably, is less able to free itself from dominance by organisational structures, and the reason here is its dependence for information and advice on the civil service (which is, of course, in turn related symbiotically to the technostructure and the mature corporation). The conclusion then follows that the executive should itself be weakened relative to the legislative branch; for clearly 'no one can appeal with confidence for vital therapy to the local doctor if he serves even more devotedly as the local undertaker'.[49]

(ii) America must have a radical party and does not have this alternative at the moment, as Galbraith pointed out in an essay written for the Fabian Society: 'The political left in Britain is roughly co-terminous with a political party. In the United States it is a part of a party which for historical reasons (as well as for no reasons at all) includes nominally its most implacable enemies, the *ante bellum* and even pre-historic southern wing.'[50]

The Democratic Party in the United States is burdened with a group of right-wingers 'whose beliefs are wholly at odds with the avowed convictions of the rest of the Party'[51] and thus anachronistic and even 'wildly irrational' in its composition. Southern re-actionaries frustrate the reforms which radicals are anxious to initiate, generate a situation where the American voter is confronted with a choice between two conservative parties (and a genuine conservative will always prefer the genuine article in any case) and present the young and the radical with the option of either voting for the worst enemies of the young and the radical or becoming estranged from the Establishment and dropping out of the System (while blacks have the additional dilemma of having to decide between Republicans always obedient to the priorities imposed by the corporate interest[52] and Southern Democrats like John L. McMillan and Jamie Whitten, men neither of whom 'even believes that blacks should vote'[53]).

The only solution is for the Democratic Party to exclude its conservatives (to expel 'the Southern warlords and white supre-macists'[54]). In this way it will become able to offer the voter a genuine and radical alternative and hence demonstrate that social reform *is* possible within the framework of the existing political system. It is, after all, difficult not to become alienated when a vote for either party is a vote for reaction.

(iii) The seniority system in Congress must be ended. In order to 'disestablish the committee mandarinate', officers such as committee chairmen should not be appointed on the basis of length of service but elected by secret ballot held at regular intervals. A

gerontocrat who can count on automatic re-election to positions of
eminence and authority will have little incentive to keep in touch
with public opinion; and his intelligence will in any case have been
dulled through lengthy exposure to bureaucratic truth (such
confusion via conditioning being at its worst where men have been
too long in contact with Pentagon and State Department: 'Here the
pseudosophistication derived from association with generals, dip-
lomats and spooks most radically divorces a man from reality'[55]).
What America needs is 'strong and skeptical political leadership',[56]
but this can hardly be expected to come from senior Congressmen
like John Stennis ('an unwavering spokesman for the military') or
L. Mendel Rivers ('a parliamentary lapdog of the Pentagon') who
clearly have 'a knee-jerk response to the military establishment'.[57]
Rather than acting as watchdogs to check and correct potential
distortions stemming from bureaucratic interest and bureaucratic
truth, such men become symbiotically linked to the needs of the
planners (as where endorsement of new defence technology not only
gives apparent legitimacy to the goals of organisation but also
means heightened prestige for legislators known to be associated
with the cause of national security and may lead to additional
weapons contracts in their constituencies[58]), respect 'what the
leaders say'[59] and squash bright young reformers until they learn to
'get along by going along'.[60]

Expectation of benefit accompanied by conviction and commitment explains why the Armed Services Committees 'are now, with
the exception of a few members, a rubber stamp for the military
power',[61] and, more generally, why Congressional committees have
become the mouthpiece through which the 'organised voice'[62] of
the military–industrial complex makes itself heard in Washington.
Description, fortunately, leads to prescription: 'No effort, including
an attack on the seniority system itself, should be spared to oust the
present functionaries and to replace them with acute and
independent-minded members.'[63]

(iv) The public regulatory bodies must be reformed, for they too
are at present symbiotically linked to a surprising and excessive
extent to the very industries that they nominally regulate:
'Regulatory bodies, like the people who comprise them, have a
marked life cycle. In youth they are vigorous, aggressive, evangelis-
tic, and even intolerant. Later they mellow, and in old age – after a
matter of ten or fifteen years – they become, with some exceptions,
either an arm of the industry they are regulating or senile.'[64] Such

sterility may well be the result of fear: since the mature corporation is popularly identified with the national interest and with technological progress, the regulatory body may become compliant so as to avoid criticism and scrutiny of itself.[65]

The solution here is in two parts. First, 'required is a consolidated regulatory body for all regulated industries. Like the Courts it would then be beyond the control of any single industry.'[66] Second, this consolidated body should remain under the watchful eye of sensitive radical politicians unwilling to subordinate themselves to the goals and needs of bureaucrats, public or private.

(v) The public must get involved in politics, for public opinion is a powerful weapon: 'We may lay it down as a law that, without public criticism, all governments look much better and are much worse.'[67] Such criticism in a free society is particularly powerful since dissent is buttressed by the franchise. Specifically, an enlightened electorate must be persuaded to vote for radical and progressive Democrats actively committed to 'planning that reflects not the planning but the public purpose'[68]; must demand from candidates for office a pledge to vote against the seniority system and to resist military programmes; and must quite concretely insist (since vague and general assurances often turn out to be mere 'verbal cloaks for inaction') that candidates solemnly promise to withhold their vote in the Democratic caucus 'if the effect is to put Mendel Rivers, John McMillan, John Stennis, Richard Russell and James Eastland into their present positions of power.'[69] These men are indifferent to 'the proper role of the legislature' and consequently 'will be better at home'.[70]

Because of public opinion, even the most insincere and opportunistic of politicians can be made to serve the public interest, and that is why domestic pressure groups devoted to those ideas which represent the 'rational view' of 'men of goodwill'[71] must be formed in order to countervail the power of the 'men who want to retreat to the eighteenth century'.[72] These pressure groups will be led not by economists but by the educational and scientific estate, by the 'learned and sensible men'[73] whose professional responsibility it is to win converts to good causes. Their efforts will be rewarded, for a pressure group in a democratic society can count on the fact that virtually any politician will 'take an earnest and principled stand on their behalf once they are really popular. But not before.'[74]

III AMERICAN SOCIALISM

Galbraith believes that the American problem is not too many bureaucrats but too few leaders of the calibre of John Kennedy: 'The Federal Executive in Washington and the good, grey American bureaucracy is not a negligible thing. Given the kind of leadership it hasn't had lately, it is capable of great things.'[75] To men with Kennedy's grasp of ideas, breadth of information, powers of concentration and reforming zeal, Galbraith recommends a 'new socialism' the precise nature of which may be considered under two headings, regulation and support.

(a) Regulation

Galbraith's proposals in *American Capitalism* appeared so anti-statist that Joan Robinson accused him of 'rebunking *laisser-faire*'[76] by seeking to limit State intervention to the creation and defence of positions of countervailing power. His argument in 1952 (as we saw in Chapter 4) was in essence this: 'Given the existence of private market power in the economy, the growth of countervailing power strengthens the capacity of the economy for autonomous self-regulation and thereby lessens the amount of over-all government control or planning that is required or sought.'[77] In the quarter century following *American Capitalism*, however, Galbraith in his pursuit of a balanced society became progressively more interventionist, and has drawn attention in particular to six potential instruments of public policy:

(i) *Restrictive practices legislation.* Galbraith notes that anti-trust laws in the United States are nowadays no more that 'a charade',[78] but seems to regard concentrated power as both inevitable (since advanced technology and heavy capital investment make large size indispensable) and beneficent (since large size means technological advance and higher productivity and thus some combination of higher wages and lower prices than would have obtained in less concentrated markets; and since giant corporations serving organisational goals expand sales where the classical monopolist for reasons of entrepreneurial profit would have sought to make output more scarce). It is in any case not feasible to break up all large producers in the American economy into smaller enterprises: the giants are simply too numerous. Restrictive practices legislation should therefore remain in existence, but its role (save where abuse of power is truly flagrant) should be passive and its function confined essentially to a watching brief.

(ii) Nationalisation. In *American Capitalism* Galbraith recommended nationalisation of industries where the presence of natural monopoly is matched by the absence of opportunity to develop countervailing power (e.g. the railways) or where private-sector response is demonstrably unrelated to social need (e.g. the provision of low-cost housing).[79] By the late 1960s, however, he had become concerned about the problem of defence-related industries (and specifically about specialised weapons firms such as Lockheed, Thiokol, General Dynamics, North American Rockwell, Aerospace, Grumman and others, which were private in name but public in practice, being heavily dependent on government for financial aid and guaranteed markets) and in 1969 informed readers of the *New York Times Magazine* that 'The Big Defense Firms are Really Public Firms and Should be Nationalized'.[80] He restated the point four years later in *Economics and the Public Purpose* as follows: 'As a rough rule a corporation (or conglomerate subsidiary) doing more than half of its business with the government should be converted into a full public corporation.'[81] Finally, and completing his move to the Left, Galbraith in 1974 announced his conversion to the idea of public ownership of all corporations where the shareholder had become a 'purely passive recipient of income' and where management in consequence had developed into a 'self-governing, self-perpetuating bureaucracy'.[82] Realising, of course, that half the American economy could not be nationalised at a stroke, Galbraith was prepared in the first instance to limit his shopping-list to the weapons firms, the lame ducks and the oil majors, hoping that public success in these three areas would generate a demonstration effect capable of engulfing the remainder of technostructure-dominated corporate capitalism. Success presupposes autonomy, however, and hence the new public corporations should be free on a day-to-day basis from outside directives, while still subject in the longer-run to the guidelines and goals laid down by politicians and by each firm's 'board of public auditors' (a body analogous to the old-style board of directors but including, alongside some executives, a majority comprised of 'men and women of strong public instinct'[83]). Galbraith's proposals seek to combine the advantages of autonomy with those of accountability, preserve that decentralisation of decision-making which is so attractive a feature of market capitalism and deal once and for all with functionless shareholders who reap where they never sowed and have constituted ever since the 1950s a major embarassment in the Galbraithian scheme of things.

(iii) Defence of the environment. The environment is neglected by private producers and individual consumers, and ought to be defended by measures in the form of town and country planning (to re-route a road that would uglify a beauty-spot, for example), strict legislation on environmental issues (say, to combat noise-nuisance or the use of disposable containers) and public building programmes (to replace urban blight with urban renewal, and possibly even to extend the scope for aesthetically satisfying but commercially unprofitable architectural projects).[84]

(iv) National economic planning. Coming only in the 1970s to national (in contrast to corporate) planning, it is no surprise that Galbraith does little more than state the case for a central authority charged with the twin tasks of forecasting (so as to isolate potential bottlenecks and ensure that microeconomic plans are co-ordinated and will mesh) and the specification of targets (concerning, say, optimal growth-rates or levels of unemployment). Evidently we are here confronted with a system part indicative, part imperative, for planners appear to have the power to specify ends as well as mobilize means.[85]

(v) Protection of disadvantaged minorities. Noting in 1971 (together with Edwin Kuh and Lester C. Thurow) that white males held a disproportionate number of executive posts, Galbraith and his colleagues called for a Minorities Advancement Plan specifying legally enforceable quotas for women and members of other disadvantaged minorities with respect to top jobs paying $15,000 or more per annum to executives of firms employing at least 2,000 persons. The quotas were, of course, to be related to the local labour catchment area, not the national labour-force; for whereas women are distributed fairly evenly throughout the country, blacks and certain other racial minorities are not.[86]

(vi) Macroeconomic policy. Galbraith believes that while demand-pull inflation arising in the market system could be dealt with effectively by means of traditional Keynesian techniques (to which he was in the 1930s an early convert) the same cannot be said of cost-push inflation generated within the planning system. There the only way to prevent giant corporations and their allied unions from passing pay-increases in excess of productivity changes backward to the shareholder or, more significantly, forward to the consumer, is by recourse to a complex and fully compulsory prices and incomes policy (which alongside macroeconomic stabilisation would also be expected to advance the cause of social justice by twisting the structure of administered differentials in favour of the relatively deprived). Galbraith sees no role at all for monetary policy (and recommends the pegging of the rate of interest at a permanently low level so as to subsidise borrowers, who are typically weak and thus in need of help); and he argues in addition that fiscal policy is to be used only in cases where a rise in taxes is called for (since he is hostile to any reduction in taxes to stimulate an economy in recession, and of course opposes anti-inflationary public expenditure cuts as an immoral attack on what is even at the best of times a poor starved creature).[87]

(b) Support

Galbraith believes in direct governmental support to deserving but less-commercial areas of social activity:

(i) The creative arts. Because the artist is too bohemian to accept the discipline and goals of the technostructure, because however art is a good thing which ought in an affluent society rather to blossom than to wilt, there is no substitute for State patronage to activities such as music and classical ballet, or for State scholarships to train the poets and novelists of the future.[88]

(ii) The planning system. State support to the giant corporation is indispensable, and ranges from the training of skilled manpower and the provision of roads to the underwriting of advanced technology and the promise of guaranteed markets. Galbraith in no way seeks to reduce such support, merely to alter its direction. The development of advanced weaponry, he argues, is not in the public interest ('Given a sufficient rate of technical progress, it is increasingly assumed, all the beneficiaries will be dead'[89]); other projects involving advanced technology (say, peaceful uses of nuclear energy, exploration of the sea-bed or research into ways of altering the world's weather) may well be more so.

(iii) The market system. Galbraith, aware of the existence of a dual economy even in an affluent society, proposes a number of schemes aimed at improving the bargaining power of the small and the weak. The State, he says, should assist them to form coalitions and cartels, to consolidate and merge, to limit new entry; it ought either to perform or to finance research and development on behalf of small businessmen unable to afford their own laboratories; and it must where necessary fix minimum prices and provide guaranteed markets. Nor should it neglect positions of weakness *within* the market system: since workers in small firms are all too often ununionised, overworked and underpaid, the State must impose minimum wage rates and specify minimum notice of dismissal.[90]

(iv) The welfare state. Galbraith is appalled by public poverty amidst private affluence; and, noting that the former includes 'some of the most significant and civilizing services'[91] (schools, slum-clearance, income-maintenance for the involuntarily unemployed, parks and recreational facilities, all of which by their very nature selectively discriminate in favour of the relatively deprived) while the latter includes the usual baubles and trinkets of highly developed countries, calls for redistribution of resources from private enterprise to public provision. Here yet again American socialism is lame-duck socialism, for the private sector has demonstrably defaulted in the area of welfare and the alternative to social action is evidently no action at all.

IV EVALUATION

Galbraith's theory of the political market is not an economist's approach to the making of political choices in the largest of all oligopolistic environments. Rather, it is an intelligent man's statement of belief that politicians are superior to bureaucrats and that the new socialism ought to embrace the ten categories outlined above. One ideology cannot refute another, and the purpose of this section is not to perform a demolition job on what is as valid a point of view as any other. Its purpose instead is to raise questions and present alternative hypotheses; for no theory of the political market can expect to be immune from competition. We will look first at the machinery of State itself and then at the specific reforms which Galbraith discusses.

(a) The machinery of State

Paradoxically, Galbraith himself at one point or another gives voice to many of the fears that critics of governmental intervention express when they advocate minimisation rather than maximisation of the role of politicians in social processes (and his comments are to be taken particularly seriously in view of his own extensive personal experience of how the political market actually works). Witness the following criticisms he has made of politicians quite celebrated in their day:

First, inconsistency and opportunism. In 1965, for example, William F. Buckley was standing for Mayor of New York City on so staunch a private enterprise platform that it was jokingly said he proposed to solve the refuse disposal problem by urging citizens to toss their rubbish out of the windows. Yet in order to win votes Buckley had to compromise his market-oriented principles even to the extent of promising (in order to win the Staten Island vote) that the general taxpayer would continue to subsidise the cheap five-cent fare charged on the Staten Island ferry. As Galbraith comments, 'one could weep'.[92]

A related phenomenon is the politician who postpones action as long as possible and then, as elections approach, suddenly decides on an ambitious and unrealistic scheme purely to impress the voter with his dynamism. Here we can take case of B. C. Roy, Chief Minister of West Bengal when Galbraith was in India, who unexpectedly developed an interest in low-cost housing: 'That is the trouble with Calcutta. The politicians have been trying to pull rabbits out of the hat for years. Their concern has been with creating an impression of accomplishment rather than accomplishment.'[93]

On a macroeconomic level, postponement of action can be politically desirable and economically disastrous. Should the speculative orgy of the 1920s recur, for instance, while 'the government preventatives and controls are ready' and although 'in the hands of a determined government their efficacy cannot be doubted',[94] yet deflation (implying as it does unemployment of labour and scarcity of loanable funds for business) may nonetheless be put off far too long simply because few leaders indeed are prepared to contemplate political defeat in the cause of sound but unpopular policies.

Inconsistency and opportunism are hardly endearing qualities, and the reader is to be forgiven if he cannot share Galbraith's touching faith in politicians who appear willing to jump on any bandwagon once its ability to win them votes has been adequately demonstrated: 'The gifted salesman waits until the parade is about to pass his door. Then he grabs the baton and marches out ahead.

That inspires real confidence.'[95] Such plastic men are if anything a menace unless constrained by enlightened public opinion (and Galbraith exaggerates the extent to which this can be mobilised and radicalised, particularly at the national level which is for his model the most significant) or at least by responsible forces within their own party (and Galbraith neglects the probability that the Democratic Party in America, being a conglomerate embracing employees, employers, farmers, bankers, television personalities, will prove too heterogeneous and diffuse a power-base to provide such a check).

Second, image-creation. Politicians in a democratic society tend to rely heavily on the manipulation of the hearts and minds of their countrymen through product differentiation and sales strategies (the '*contrived* build-up',[96] often deliberately synthesised and designed by skilled public relations engineers in exchange for a fee), through argument by analogy (the '*autonomous* build-up'[97] whereby success in one field, notably the field of battle, causes the electorate to anticipate success in all others and encourages would-be leaders to take advantage of such gullibility to seek responsibilities for which they are eminently unsuited), through 'Titan II rhetoric' and 'Procter and Gamble sincerity',[98] through 'third-dimension departure'[99] (the net side-stepping of both positions on a difficult question) and, of course, through the 'wordfact' ('one of the most important modern instruments of public administration'):

> The wordfact makes words a precise substitute for reality. This is an enormous convenience. It means that to say something exists is a substitute for its existence. And to say that something will happen is nearly as good as having it happen. The saving in energy is nearly total . . . Where once it was said of a statesman that he suited action to the words, now he suits the words to the action. If past action (or inaction) has failed to produce the desired result, then, by resort to wordfact, he quickly establishes that the undesired result was more desirable than the desired result.[100]

Politicians, in other words, deliberately seek to make things appear other than they are (where necessary, to mask failure, as when they identify unemployment not as a misfortune but as 'the introduction of needed and desirable slack in the system'[101]) and do not scruple to make promises which they have no intention of keeping (as when, in the 1950s, 'strong statements in favor of school integration and voting rights for Negroes' were 'a widely accepted substitute for progress'[102]). Nor is it true to say that the electorate will always recognise falsehood and ferret out deceit, for history bears witness to the frequency of successful deception and 'truly splendid fraud', as in the cases of Bernard Baruch and Douglas MacArthur: 'Both raised self-advertisement to the level of high art. Unlike such gross amateurs as Lyndon Johnson and Richard Nixon, they got away with it. No one spoke of a credibility gap; no matter how fantastic their vision of themselves, everyone accepted it.'[103]

Third, lack of information. Politicians are busy men unable to gather facts for themselves and dependent upon their advisers for predigested and filtered intelligence. Politicians, moreover, lack specialist expertise and cannot be expected to make decisions on technical questions without serious consequences (witness the fate of Nikita Krushchev, who 'was canned because of his inability to keep his hands off technical matters on which he was uninformed, including among other things hybrid corn'[104]). It would consequently be wrong to exaggerate the extent to which politicians are in fact able to act as a bulwark against bureaucratic symbiosis and bureaucratic inertia: the enemy cannot be put to rout, no matter how much the relative power of the politician is strengthened, so long as specialist advice remains essential.

Naturally, the government could try to mobilise for itself independent scientific opinion in the form of outside experts. It is not, however, certain that the RAND Corporation, the Hudson Institute or even the university-based specialist is entirely free from intellectual pollution through past association with bureaucratic truth (possibly via the mediation of the press, including 'cold war columnists' such as Joseph Alsop and Robert Novak,[105] veteran journalists whose ideological orientation is likely to ensure them symbiotic relationships with veteran civil servants). It is, moreover, likely that outside experts will have to depend heavily for classified information on bureaucrats in bodies such as the CIA and the State Department, who will as a consequence of their position have selected what data to collect, have evaluated it in accordance with their belief-system, and have decided how much to regard as top secret and how much to release. Even in the realm of economic and social policy, the very suppression of the market mechanism in a wide range of domains and the lack of direct consumer consultation is bound to make the politician ever more the prisoner of pre-selected statistics and administered truths.

Politicians, in short, cannot in all cases be expected, merely by virtue of their office, either to have adequate access to accurate information or to possess the expertise necessary to make full use of it. A man who can persuade the electorate to vote for him need not, after all, be a man with sufficient intelligence and skill to deal with the complex issues facing the nation: 'One of the oldest puzzles of politics is who is to regulate the regulators. But an equally baffling problem, which has never received the attention it deserves, is who is to make wise those who are required to have wisdom.'[106] Kennedy and Albert Speer (Hitler's 'highly intelligent arms minister'[107] whom Galbraith met in 1945 in connection with his work on the effectiveness of Allied bombing in Germany when he was in the Strategic Bombing Survey) were wise, but the same cannot be said of Dean Rusk, a Secretary of State 'singularly devoid of any desire to accomplish anything'[108]. ('The epitome of the organization man in our time was Secretary of State Dean Rusk. Few have served organization with such uncritical devotion.'[109]) or of those statesmen on the House Foreign Affairs Committee whom Galbraith describes in his novel *The Triumph* (and all of whom turn out to be either ignorant or absent[110]).

Fourth, corruption. Politicians, aware that they, like other citizens, stand financially to gain or to lose from particular policies, may make decisions with an eye to bank accounts rather than national accounts (as where President Warren G. Harding and several of his cabinet colleagues took no steps to arrest the speculative boom of the 1920s precisely because they themselves 'were making money out of it'[111] and feared personal disaster should the boom come to an end). Again, while direct bribery is becoming less common than it was in the era of the classical capitalist entrepreneur (this because the technostructure knows how difficult it is not only to make decisions but to keep secrets in a situation where dirty dealings are arranged by committees within which 'each member is his brother's auditor and watchdog'[112]; because it fears adverse publicity which would tarnish the image of men who work for prestige as well as pay; because it does not own the resources it controls or directly receive the marginal profits that result from graft, and, basically, corrupting officials 'is not something one does on a salary'[113]), nonetheless the Establishment politician has a material incentive to support organisational objectives: he receives not personal support but contracts and installations for his constituency, and these are bound to pay rich dividends when the electorate comes to show its appreciation in the usual way.[114]

Given that a cynical observer can detect in Galbraith's own work four good arguments against the centralisation of power in the hands of politicians, the question must then be posed of how Galbraith can be so confident that an enlightened and sceptical electorate will come to acknowledge the merits of men like Stevenson and Nehru and reject inferior figures like Barry Goldwater and Krishna Menon. For confident he is: the 'vast verbal fallout' of the past, he maintains, is 'certain to breed a reaction',[115] and adds that voters are already, in his view, becoming more critical and less gullible. Perhaps the sovereign consumer does behave like a pig in a pastry shop; the sovereign citizen may nonetheless be expected to behave like a paragon of virtue, voting for the man of action rather than the man of rhetoric, for higher taxes rather than bigger motor-cars.

Galbraith is confident and he must be so; for in his view in all countries 'a large number of articulate citizens' alone constitutes the watchdog of democracy. It alone protects society against the 'pious promises' of fools and hypocrites who would otherwise divorce 'talk' from 'intention', and ensures the election of omniscient and beneficent statesmen who have the public good at heart. Galbraith's optimism and enthusiasm are appealing. His confidence, unfortunately, is not contagious; for it appears in the last analysis to be rooted more deeply in sincere belief than in hard fact.

(b) Social reform

The attraction of Galbraith's ten specific proposals for State intervention is a function in considerable measure simply of personal preference. The reader may nonetheless wish to be reminded of a whole series of arguments which are to some extent concealed by what Colin Clark has called Galbraith's 'fatal fluency'.[116] Thus, for instance, if American anti-trust laws are today truly 'a charade', they could tomorrow be made less so (with respect, say, to those mergers and take-overs which give the raider security and market domination but yield no genuine economies of large scale and provide no particular incentive to expand investment in research and development), for workable competition may be a realistic target even where perfect competition is not; nationalisation is likely rather to accentuate than to resolve the problem of concentrated and bureaucratised power and does nothing to ensure that the goals and techniques of the technostructure will be radically altered (Galbraith indeed stresses that the public corporation is to be run on commercial lines and not as a public utility, a serious constraint on the powers of its in any case somewhat nebulous 'board of public auditors'); town and country planning substantially expands the role of administrative (and reduces the role of individual) decision-making (and in any case does nothing to internalise social costs imposed on all by a few); while national economic planning in the Galbraithian model (admittedly an afterthought) requires the planners not simply to forecast for micro-markets (without assisting firms to share out totals among themselves, an omission which reflects the usual Galbraithian assumption of constant and conventional shares) but also to set targets that reflect the public interest (a suggestion which raises unanswered questions concerning power, responsibility and consensus). As for protection of disadvantaged minorities, quotas, it might be argued, breed resentful accusations of a new feudalism in which status replaces achievement, and may also represent a wasteful sacrifice of efficiency to equity, at least in the case of that minority of jobs (i.e. executive posts) to which the rules are to apply; and with respect to macroeconomic policy the previous arguments concerning resentment and inefficiency (both arising from the centrally administered differentials of a prices and incomes policy) must be supplemented by an additional argument, the probable failure of policy to attain its objectives (since unions may refuse to cooperate in measures which depart from free collective bargaining, and since monetary policy is to be scrapped and fiscal policy seriously weakened). Then, State support to the arts, precisely because it represents the decision of an élite to spend public revenues in a way that the majority of ordinary citizens demonstrably would not, is open to the accusations normally levelled against a polity divorced from its society, and may in any case mean political defeat (to say nothing of political directives and criteria); State support to the planning system (even if for peacetime rather than military purposes) hardly protects weak firms against strong ones (although it does protect lame-duck corporations against the cold wind of competition which might otherwise have compelled them to release resources for more viable undertakings) and may not even be an unmixed blessing for the powerful themselves (Professor Demsetz has tested Galbraith's claim that the defence industries are optimally placed to plan their future with confidence because the State is their principal customer and reports that, for the period 1949–64, a sample of the relevant US shares tended to fluctuate *more* rather than *less* than did an equivalent number of alternative shares, randomly selected[117]); State support to the market system is unlikely to satisfy advocates of small business (who will regard measures such as socially sponsored research and development projects as but a first step in the right direction, and measures such as the minimum wage as a first step in the wrong one, particularly since Galbraith himself accepts with equanimity that this latter proposal is *ceteris paribus* bound to drive out labour and actually reduce output in the small firm sector[118]), nor indeed to satisfy the consumer interest (as where fixed price-floors and guaranteed markets to small farmers raise the prices of bread in the shops, a state of affairs unlikely to minimise social tensions); and State support to the otherwise impoverished welfare services is bound to upset all those who reject the determinism of the residual supplier argument, whether their ideological orientation be collectivist (as in the case of thinkers such as Titmuss, who believe that the welfare state is not imposed by circumstance but emerges proudly as the product of altruistic social values and a deep sense of community) or individualist (as in the case of thinkers such as Spencer, who believe that schools and hospitals, like cabbages and aspirins, ought to and can be supplied by the enlightened self-interest of private enterprise and allocated by the invisible hand of the market mechanism). All in all, therefore, Galbraith's ten specific proposals for State intervention are topics for extended debate and it is salutary to remember that a case against the political market can also be made out, even if perhaps never quite as entertainingly as in the work of Professor Galbraith.

7 The Emancipation of Belief

Galbraith believes that social goals need to be revised, and that the precondition for such revision is the emancipation of belief from the chains of outdated ideology.

In Section I of this chapter we will examine Galbraith's views on the relationship between mind and matter, while in Sections II, III and IV we will look in some detail at those social groups which have the function of emancipating belief. In Section V we will offer a critical evaluation of Galbraith's views on ideology and social progress.

I THE STATUS OF BELIEF

Galbraith is convinced that the fight for freedom must commence at the level of ideas, not at the level of things: 'If belief is the source of power, the attack must be on belief. Law cannot anticipate understanding.'[1] The antidote to a false perception of modern conditions is thus in the first instance reasoned argument: 'One does not suppress neo-classical economics; one shows its tendentious function and seeks to provide a substitute. One does not prohibit advertising; one resists its persuasion. One does not legislate against science or engineering; one sees their eminence in relation to the arts as the contrivance of the planning system.'[2] People must become aware that they live in 'the thraldom of a myth'[3] since awareness is the means to emancipation from its dangers: 'Knowledge of the forces by which one is constrained is the first step towards freedom.'[4] Ideas, in other words, have consequences, and thus popular understanding has the power to alter the direction in which society is evolving: 'No one who believes in ideas and their advocacy can ever persuade himself that they are uninfluential. . . . I have hopes that popular understanding will reverse some of the less agreeable tendencies of the industrial system and invalidate, therewith, the predictions that proceed from these tendencies.'[5]

Galbraith is also convinced, however, that the scope for idealism is severely restricted by the momentum inherent in matter: 'It is part of man's pride that he makes economic policy; in fact, in economic affairs, he normally adjusts his actions, within a comparatively narrow range of choice, to circumstances.'[6] Even in politics, 'we need hardly remind ourselves that political issues are made not by parties and politicians but by circumstance',[7] and that means by the state of technology and its economic applications: 'The imperatives of technology and organization, not the images of ideology, are what determine the shape of economic society.'[8] Material phenomena have laws of motion of their own, and the ideologist should remember that 'for being right . . . it is better to have the support of events than of the higher scholarship'[9]: 'In social matters, critics are an interim phenomenon. Given a little time, circumstances will prove you either right or wrong.'[10]

There thus appears to be a contradiction in Galbraith's theory of social change between his idealism and his materialism, his reformism and his determinism. On the one hand he appears to be arguing that ideas have consequences, while on the other he appears to be maintaining that consequences are primary and thought is afterthought. The contradiction is more apparent than real, however; and the reason is Galbraith's dynamic dialectical method which (like that of Karl Marx) derives both the evolution and the perception of *what ought to be* from unresolved conflicts within the matrix of *what is*. The method involves the creation, apperception and transcendence of contradictions in the course of social change; and serves to demonstrate, in Galbraith's model, that the solutions inescapably will be those that he himself both favours and predicts. The key link is thought: the situation generates the problem, the problem the perception, the perception the solution, as will become clear once we have examined forces operating in three important spheres of contemporary American capitalism.

II THE PLANNING SYSTEM

In this section we will consider four self-transcending contradictions arising within the planning system itself.

First, there are contradictions associated with macroeconomic imbalance. In a recession, no matter how much in theory a politician opposes Keynesian and other interventionist measures to stimulate aggregate demand, he will still not seriously contemplate *laissez-faire*: given that market imbalance is not self-correcting, his real and only choice is 'whether or not to commit political suicide'.[11] Similarly, in a situation of cost-push inflation there is simply no alternative to a prices and incomes policy. Controls were introduced in the Second World War not so much as the result of careful deliberation and conscious choice as because 'circumstances appeared to offer no other course'[12]; and the force of events also led to the introduction by Kennedy of 'guideposts' in 1961[13] and the imposition by Nixon of a complete freeze in 1971 (a freeze which even extended to executive remuneration).[14] The technostructure will naturally resent interference with its autonomy to set prices and incomes; but it will nonetheless come to welcome State action as complementary to corporate planning techniques. After all, the management of specific demand (the demand for the firm's product) is more difficult when the general price index is rising, as the consumer is then likely mistakenly to confuse real with money values and buy less of the product (in the belief that it is dearer) rather than more (as the growth-objective of the firm requires). Controls, moreover, are the ideal accompaniment to oligopoly, since ceilings ensure that competitors will not unexpectedly alter prices; while planning of pay structures gives the corporation security from the push of the unions. As for the unions themselves, while understandably wary of pay-policy lest it impose wages lower than those that would have been set by collective bargaining and fearful lest government regulation make unions redundant and accelerate their decline, they too will come to see that they on balance benefit from planning rather than chance (if only because controls eliminate the danger of a rise in prices eroding the purchasing power of a previous rise in wages and thus reducing real gains). Controls, in summary, are both inevitable and acceptable. They are also socially desirable, and for this reason inflationary pressures themselves are an emancipatory force in Galbraith's model.

Second, there are contradictions associated with the environment, since the planning system imposes on society certain costs which it does not itself cover and which become greater and more visible as economic growth progresses. More cars mean more pollution and more congestion in a free enterprise system, while land development can well mean aesthetic disaster if left a private prerogative. Understandably, even conservatives like Barry Goldwater have under the pressure of circumstances opted at least partially for town and country planning: 'Early this year, he lent his name to an effort to socialize Camelback Mountain, which abuts the Goldwater backyard. He wanted to turn it into a public park and thus prevent unsightly real estate development by the American free private-enterprise system.'[15] Public discontent has already induced Hawaii and Vermont to ban highway advertising[16], and has also led to controls on DDT, non-degradable detergents and supersonic aircraft.[17] It has stimulated de-pollution campaigns and created an atmosphere in which the citizenry is prepared to finance them.

Third, the contradiction between 'what is taught and what exists'[18] is helping to discredit traditional theories of supply and demand: 'When belief is stretched too far, it snaps; the doctrine is rejected. The same is true of refinement without relevance. It comes, sooner or later, to seem but a game. Not surprisingly in recent years the neo-classical model has been losing its hold – especially on the minds of younger scholars.'[19] Textbook economics, indeed, confronted with an ever-increasing divergence between theory and practice, positively adds to 'frustration and conflict'[20] by presenting an ideal (albeit stereotyped and fictitious) against which present-day shortcomings may be evaluated. Discontent is the result, for 'if we foster great expectations, we must count on deep disillusion'.[21]

Consider first the case of supply. Traditional theories, being couched in terms of a profit-oriented entrepreneur, neglect the devolution of decision-making from owners to corporate bureaucrats with goals of their own not unlike those of State bureaucrats. Traditional theories, moreover, being couched in terms of individualism, neglect the collectivism and organic unity of the technostructure. In a sense Galbraith is saying that the true ideology of modern capitalism was identified by his teachers at school in Canada when they discouraged team sports in order to protect the child 'from the socialist interdependence inculcated by the team spirit'[22]: 'Few things, by commonly advocated standards, are so bad for the youngster of impressionable age as team sports. Instead of causing him to think first of his own self-interest, they turn his mind to the problem of the group. He ceases to be an individualist and becomes a mere cog in a social machine.'[23] The football team, like the modern technostructure, plays as a unit, conforms to group discipline, and enjoys its prizes in common. As Galbraith's fictional creation, Mr Allston Wheat, noted in his study of 'Athletics and Americanism', the first rules for college football were drawn up in 1867, the same year as the publication of Marx's *Capital*. Mr Wheat was quick to see the connection: 'If you are looking for the real advance guard for modern Communism, you should go to the field-houses and the football stadiums.'[24] Allston Wheat is a figure of fun. There is, however, a germ of truth in his crusade; and it is not only in the football team that the subordination of the individual to the group is today to be found and perceived to be found.

Consider now the case of demand. Here orthodox theory no longer adequately explains the problems which people find most urgent. The public is sceptical that it really chose trivial and often undependable gadgets produced by quasi-fraudulent research and development in preference to improved social balance: 'When houses and health care are unavailable and male deodorants are abundant, the notion of a benign response to public wants begins to buckle under the strain.'[25] The public is increasingly aware, moreover, that many consumer goods are unhealthy (such as cigarettes and alcohol), defective (witness the influence of Ralph Nader's book *Unsafe at any Speed* and the spread of the consumerist movement), unavailable (an argument for economic planning to eliminate bottlenecks) or the spin-off of socially financed but eminently dangerous programmes (such as the development of new weaponry). People are becoming ever more conscious of the manipulative function of advertising, annoyance with which is already being reflected in the United States in the success of cable television; and perhaps in future the public will even be willing similarly to pay a higher price for newspapers in order there too to free itself from the exaggerations of corporate publicity. An awareness of manipulation discredits the individualist belief in consumer sovereignty, diminishes the prestige of both commodities and corporations and reduces the efficacy of demand-management itself; for nowadays even 'the merest child watching television dismisses the health and status-giving claims of a breakfast cereal as "a commercial" '.[26] To those 'who sense what is happening', it is clear that the general public is coming to grasp the reality of producer sovereignty: 'In the United States and the other industrial societies, it is a commonplace explanation of tension and discontent that the individual feels himself in the grip of large, impersonal forces whose purposes he senses to be hostile and in relation to which he feels helpless.'[27] The individual increasingly feels other-directed and in the grip of organisations public (such as the Pentagon) and private (such as General Motors) which 'have power to pursue purposes of their own that are different from those of the consumer or citizen'.[28] The perception of other-directedness is a valuable step in the emancipation of belief.

Fourth, there are contradictions within the planning system such that American Big Business is becoming increasingly socialist in nature, if by socialism we mean 'a position by the State in the capital structure or plant of an industry or firm that is large enough to provide or portend major social influence or control'.[29]

Consider first the example of the Penn Central Railroad, where the revolt against private ownership and *laissez-faire* was led not by the ideologues, nor by the classical proletariat, nor even by the customers (the passengers and the shippers), but by the executives of this, the largest transport company in the United States. The reason was that the company was unable to pay its debts and faced bankruptcy proceedings. Pushed on by a consortium of banker-creditors, 'the railroad executives turned to the State. . . . This dramatic rush to socialism won the initial approval of the Republican Administration.'[30] The cause of socialism was in short successfully espoused by a coalition of executives, bankers and conservative politicians once private enterprise in a crucial sector had gone irremediably into the red. And the process of socialisation is self-feeding. Washington will soon learn that efficiency and rationalisation of the railways (to say nothing of their survival) depend on State participation, and the public that it has at last found an accountable authority to which it can successfully appeal for better service: 'Once the government has a firm stake in Penn Central, the public will start demanding better and cleaner trains that also arrive. And shippers will demand that their freight is delivered. The government, as those who fear socialism have long warned, is extremely vulnerable to such pressure. Public funds will be spent to improve service. And as things get better on the Penn Central, people will want similar changes on the other roads.'[31]

Take now, as another example of creeping socialism, the case of Lockheed. It too demonstrates how our contemporary ideology is out of date; for whereas ideology postulates individualism, Lockheed is in fact both collectively owned (by an amorphous mass of dispersed shareholders) and collectively administered (by a team of bureaucrats). Ideology, moreover, postulates political *laissez-faire*; and yet Lockheed enjoys a special relationship with the State, which now provides much of its fixed plant and working capital and serves as its principal customer. Defence is one of several 'already extensively socialized industries',[32] linked to the State by ties of symbiosis.[33] Despite this blurring of the line between public and private, however, Lockheed in the late 1960s was unable to pay its bills: 'Like the Penn Central, Lockheed wants the government even more in.'[34] Indeed, the technostructure of this giant corporation was desperate for public participation once it learned that the financial community would only lend if the government extended over three times the amount in loans, gifts and guarantees: the pressure of the banks for a measure of socialism is clearly more powerful than that of radicals and demonstrators. What remains is simply an ideological tidying-up operation as result of which government control can be joined to government finance; for in the 1960s, although 'the management of the Lockheed Corporation was inadequate in a uniquely expensive way', and although 'almost all of its orders came from the government and the government was guaranteeing its debt', nonetheless 'the right of the corporation to run its affairs in its own way went largely unchallenged'.[35]

Take finally, as a third example of incipient socialism, the situation on the New York Stock Exchange in the late 1960s. The problem there was that an investor who left stock with his broker for trading purposes or bought on margin with the intention of re-selling often made a financial loss should the market slump since brokers on occasion became illiquid and unable to restore to their customers the money and securities left with them. Wall Street, sympathising with the distress of the speculator subject to insecurity in the service of free enterprise, consequently set up the Securities Investor Protection Corporation to compensate the customers and creditors of failed brokers, and obtained for this body a governmental guarantee of one billion dollars to help cushion private speculators against losses arising from the risks they take. So much for the myth that the Stock Exchange is an intervention-free perfect market! The next step, moreover, is likely to be even more dramatic: when several of the larger brokers fail, 'the government will step in to conserve their assets against the claims it has paid. There will be strong pressure to minimize hardship and unemployment by keeping the firms going. The government will oblige—the familiar yielding to pressure again. Presently other firms will fail and the government will find itself in a dominant position on the Street and in the Exchange.'[36] Judging from this sample scenario, 'no old-fashioned socialist ever had a better idea for getting a foothold on Wall Street'.[37]

Taking these three examples together, what is striking is that executives, bankers, brokers and speculators behaved virtually as if they were consciously seeking to discredit market capitalism. The Penn Central, for instance, paid dividends to shareholders (admittedly a must for the security of the technostructure) with cash that was needed for safety and efficiency of operations, and even wasted capital on real estate promotion in Texas, Florida and California. Lockheed made wildly erroneous cost-calculations ('The tactic of the new socialists at Lockheed was clear. They were out to make the Post Office look good and they succeeded.'[38]) And brokers subjected their clients to delays and malversation of funds (abuses which lend themselves 'especially well to propaganda designed to discredit the system'[39]).

What has happened, in short, is that threatened bankruptcy or continued losses in key but weak industries have led to State intervention and even to State takeover. For this reason, socialists should not be too hostile to the occasional recession: 'So long as they were making profits, the railroads, Lockheed, Pan Am, Franklin National were flagships of the private enterprise system. Once the profits turned into losses they became the highly deserving wards of the State. . . . If the present troubles of the other investor-owned utilities continue, this ideological change could become a torrent.'[40] And the imposition of lame-duck socialism is more than just an American phenomenon: 'As in the United States, so in other countries. In Britain there is strong objection to public ownership except, as in the case of Rolls Royce, where private miscalculation has brought disaster. Then it is favored, and urgently, by conservatives. The Italians have built a large public sector of the economy, by no means unsuccessful, mostly from the failures of private enterprise.'[41] The owl of Minerva evidently flies at dusk and then only under the pressure of circumstance; but at least it does fly.

III THE MILITARY–INDUSTRIAL COMPLEX

In this section we will examine the contradictions arising within the

military–industrial complex which are favourable to the emancipation of belief and the coming of the millenium. Here an
interesting lesson may perhaps be learnt from the Great Wall of
China, which was built by a foolish Emperor at an enormous cost in
men and materials: 'Although the cost was heavy, the Emperor
would not compromise where national security was concerned. He
knew that one should not trifle when survival is at stake. The people
did not agree, and the Emperor was overthrown, not by the
barbarians from the North but by the Chinese peasants who wanted
a reordering of national priorities.'[42] One may confidently expect
the same fate that befell the Emperor to overtake the Pentagon, the
State Department and General Dynamics, and for the following
reasons:

To begin with, concern about the complex is expressed not just by
student radicals but by those respectable businessmen who are left
out in the cold when it comes to benefits but not when it comes to
costs. After all, defence contracts are not shared out equally and
evenly between firms but are redistributive in favour of the strong:
'In 1968, the hundred largest defense contractors had more than
two-thirds (67·4 per cent) of all the defense business and the smallest
fifty of these had no more in the aggregate than General Dynamics
and Lockheed. . . . For the vast majority of businessmen the only
association with the defense business is through the taxes they pay.
Not even a subcontract comes their way.'[43] Clearly, the willingness
of the smaller businessman to sign blank cheques in favour of large
organisations is not without limits, and imbalance is bound to breed
resentment.

Those businessmen not in the military–industrial complex must,
moreover, bear still more burdens on its behalf: 'They must operate
in communities that are starved for revenue, where, in consequence,
their business is exposed to disorder and violence and where
materials and manpower are preempted by the defense contractors.
They must also put up with inflation, high interest rates and
regulation on overseas investment occasioned by defense spending.'[44] Nowadays, following race riots and crime waves, there is a
new awareness of poverty and the problems of the inner city; a
widespread acceptance that government spending on social balance
is not only desirable in its own right but actually in the interest of the
business community itself; and an increasing recognition that 'if it
weren't for the exaggerated demands of the Pentagon, federal tax
revenues would be available in volume to aid the cities and to ease

the pressure on the property tax.'[45] Nowadays, too, even Wall Street acknowledges that militarism is simply not good business: 'Legend has it marching Americans against Communism in Indo-China, defending American imperial interests everywhere else and holding the line against socialism in the United States. Somewhat inconsistently it provided the largest part of Senator Eugene McCarthy's financial support when he ran for the Presidency in 1968.'[46] The demonstrated incompatibility of American capitalism with the war in Vietnam illustrates forcefully the inevitability of the negation of the negation.

Yet another welcome indication that contemporary ideology is conveniently self-transcending is to be found in the geographical concentration of defence contracts: 'In 1967 three favored states out of fifty – California and New York and Texas – received one-third. Ten states accounted for a full two-thirds.'[47] Galbraith recognises that, quite understandably, 'many Senators and Congressmen are slow to criticize expenditures in their districts even though for most of their supporters the cost vastly exceeds the gain.'[48] He notes with glee, however, that, because of the unequal geographical distribution of contracts, 'in all but a handful of cases the Congressman or Senator who votes for military spending is voting for the enrichment of people he does not represent at the expense of those who elect him.'[49] Clearly, in certain circumstances political democracy can be expected to generate political opposition to the military–industrial complex. This presupposes, however, that the momentum of the Cold War ideology can first be arrested, as otherwise politicians will be too petrified by the fear of being thought 'soft on Communism' to act in the pecuniary self-interest of their constituents. Fortunately, here too circumstances are propitious, for Cold War attitudes are so much on the decline that the national state of mind when they were at their peak seems to us today to be ludicrous.[50]

The decline in Cold War panic is the result of experience. For one thing, whereas the Communist imperium once seemed monolithic, it has increasingly become (and is increasingly perceived to be) almost as pluralistic as the West: 'Moscow and Peking barely keep the peace. Fear in Czechoslovakia, Yugoslavia, and Roumania is not of the capitalist enemy but the great Communist friend.'[51] A set of quarrelling partners is naturally a much less formidable enemy than a unified bloc.

Then, too, experience in countries such as Britain has shown military spending to be capable of considerable pruning – without provoking the apocalypse – when economic pressures made drastic reductions inescapable: 'So it was with the Singapore presence; military necessity required it until the balance of payments could no longer sustain it. Then it went without damage. So it was with the F-III, the swing-wing aerial dinosaur. The RAF could not exist without it until the economy could no longer afford it. Thereafter both the RAF and Britain survived.'[52]

In the Third World, moreover, the Communist danger has turned out to be a paper tiger: 'The Soviets have had no more success than has capitalism in penetrating and organizing the backward countries of the world.'[53] The image of East as well as West is tarnished by technostructures and bureaucracies, and there is little evidence that the Eastern countries have attempted by force to impose their ideology on the uncommitted: 'The Communist powers are cautious – rather more cautious perhaps than the government of the United States – about risking disaster in pursuit of an idea.'[54] Experience has taught a lesson that might well have been anticipated, namely that developing countries are not particularly interested in the choice between capitalism and Communism: 'That alternatives to capitalism only become interesting after there is capitalism (and associated industrialization) was eloquently affirmed by Marx more than a century ago. That capitalism is only an issue if there is capitalism is a proposition not, in its essentials, difficult to grasp.'[55] And even if they were, America's vital interests need not be affected by a change of system in a foreign country: 'We have also found, as in the nearby case of Cuba, that a country can go Communist without any overpowering damage.'[56]

Finally, the military–industrial complex will be defeated by virtue of the simple fact that all bureaucracies are unable to respond effectively to attack: 'A bureaucracy under attack is a fortress with thick walls but fixed guns.'[57] For this reason, 'Vietnam will be the graveyard of the old policy',[58] since it exposed the rigid and unrealistic assumptions underlying bureaucratic truth and revealed the vulnerability of bureaucrats once they are put on the defensive: 'Organization could not come up with any effective response to its critics on Vietnam. The old slogans – we must resist worldwide Communist aggression, we must not reward aggression, we must stand by our brave allies – were employed not only after repetition had robbed them of all meaning but after they had been made ludicrous by events.'[59]

The painful catalyst of the Vietnam War thus served to break the inertia of self-perpetuating organisational truth by rendering bureaucrats helpless in the face of criticism and by compelling politicians to lead rather than blindly follow the civil service. It is, of course, regrettable that America 'paid heavily for the myth of the old policy in Vietnam'.[60] Fortunately, however, 'the lessons – the dangers of unlimited commitment, the dangers in supporting governments that are unsupported by their people, the limits of military solutions, the healthy skepticism of our own people where official truth is involved – are all brilliantly clear. Perhaps these inhospitable jungles were well designed to stimulate a more liberal, more rational, more discriminating, more collectively motivated and somewhat less paranoiac view of our mission in the world.'[61]

The prestige of the military–industrial complex was high in the 1940s (in the aftermath of the Second World War) and in the 1950s (in the era of the Cold War). Its prestige fell in the 1960s due to a series of foreign policy disasters (ranging from the Bay of Pigs to Vietnam by way of the Dominican Republic and China) which were bound inevitably to result from the inflexibilities and inaccuracies of bureaucratic truth. These disasters have discredited the complex, made politicians sceptical about bureaucratic advice, and even tinged the military itself with failure, for whereas in the 1950s the military was identified with the folk heroes of the Second World War (men such as Eisenhower, Marshall and Bradley), in the 1960s it was identified with the fiasco in Vietnam: 'Its credibility has been deeply damaged by its fatal association with the bureaucratic truths of that war – with the long succession of defeats that became victories, the victories that became defeats and brilliant actions that did not signify anything at all. In the fifties it required courage for a civilian to challenge Eisenhower on military matters. Anyone is allowed to doubt the omniscience of General William C. Westmoreland.'[62] Discredited bureaucratic truths lead to a generation of discredited generals, and prove yet again that the military–industrial complex has a built-in auto-destructive mechanism.

IV THE EDUCATIONAL AND SCIENTIFIC ESTATE

In this section we will examine the manifest and the latent functions of mass education and its expansion and demonstrate how the essential contradictions inherent in the education industry constitute important forces working for social progress.

The manifest function of education is the formation of skilled manpower and disciplined intelligence; and, since it is widely accepted that technocrat and bureaucrat are only able to perform their duties because of their trainers, it would appear that schools and particularly universities have to a considerable extent become

preparatory academies for the technostructure. The great prestige of the pure and applied sciences and mathematics in modern times, and the support accorded them, reflect the needs of the technostructure. The ample sums available for research and related graduate training in these areas reflect specific adaptation to such need, whereas the lesser prestige and lesser support for the arts and humanities suggest their inferior role. No modern university administration would insist, in fact as distinct from speech, that the study of the theatre, fine arts or *Beowulf* had the same claim to funds in the same ammounts as an electronic accelerator or the computer centre. Such is the influence of the industrial system.[63]

The demand for educational facilities and their expansion, because it originates to a substantial degree within the planning system and reflects the needs of the powerful for the crucial scarce factor of modern industry, is better catered-for by the State than the demand for, say, museums, mental hospitals and old age pensions, although these alternative services are no more adequately provided via the invisible magic of free enterprise and the market.[64] The government is willing to fund facilities such as for training because it appreciates that education is an investment which, by improving the productivity of human capital, makes the nation richer: 'Studies by Theodore Schultz, among others in the United States, have recently shown that outlays for education may bring large increases in production. . . . They have shown that a dollar or a rupee invested in the intellectual improvement of human beings will often bring a greater increase in national income than a dollar or a rupee devoted to railways, dams, machine tools, or other tangible capital goods.'[65] When it comes to the expansion of the educational sector, in short, the government is unusually sensitive to the arguments of the economic lobby: 'It is the vanity of educators that they shape the educational system to their preferred image. They may not be without influence but the decisive force is the economic system. What the educator believes is latitude is usually latitude to respond to economic need.'[66]

The latent function is somewhat less conservative, somewhat less committed to the perpetuation of the *status quo*; and it arises because educators (and despite the fact that they train the strategic and vital specialists upon whom modern industry, technological advance and planning depend) are also the guardians of 'the values and goals of educated men – those that serve not the production of goods and associated planning but the intellectual and artistic development of man'.[67] The latent function of mass education and its expansion is evidently the emancipation of belief, and it operates in the following way:

Firstly, education integrates as well as enriches. Once, 'when capital was the key to economic success, social conflict was between the rich and the poor'.[68] In recent times, however, 'education has become the difference that divides'.[69] Understandably, in an era when highly trained manpower is the most prestigious input and when the 'relevant class distinction in our time'[70] is that between the more-certified and the less-certified, education increases social mobility and relieves social tensions. Education is simultaneously an attack on poverty (since good jobs in modern industry tend to go to the skilled and the qualified), and also an attack on juvenile delinquency; for 'the social, athletic, dramatic, and like attractions of the school . . . together with the other recreational opportunities of the community'[71] at the very least keep poor children off the streets and distract them from creative destruction.

Education can, moreover, help a community to combat structural unemployment. The need to retrain can, in a dynamic economy, affect any group in the working population; and even the technostructure itself, being highly qualified but lacking flexibility, is not secure from the obsolescence of specific skills and thus the need to acquire new ones. Previous education at least increases a man's malleability and receptiveness to additional training, and thus maximises his potential lifetime mobility (both occupational and geographical). It ensures that he will be able to remain an active member of the national family rather than a stranger on the outside looking in.

Secondly, education instills 'comprehension and scepticism' in students (even in those training to be scientists and engineers) and thus ensures 'that there will be systematic questioning of the beliefs impressed by the industrial system'.[72] A man whose intellect has been trained and who has been taught to think and reason critically for himself (even if the overt objective of his education was to equip him with useful skills) is more likely to see through the fictions of demand-management and want-creation than is a man without education: 'Thus the paradox. The economy for its success requires organized public bamboozlement. At the same time it nurtures a growing class which feels itself superior to such bamboozlement and deplores it as intellectually corrupt.'[73] Whatever it is, education by its very nature is ill-suited to serve the ends of social conditioning and commercial propaganda; for simple minds, not trained ones, are 'easiest to manage',[74] and highly trained minds are often not manageable at all.

More generally, all education widens tastes and attracts attention to those cultural pursuits which are tragically neglected by the technostructure. Education, in other words, is not only consumption as well as investment, but it is a form of consumption in many ways morally superior to investment: 'The enrichment of the mind is an important as the nourishment of the body. Intellectual activity is properly pursued for its own sake; the poet, artist or writer rightfully scorns economic gain as a test of performance. Because of their tendency to apply economic calculation to refreshment of the spirit and mind, Carlyle characterized economists as the learned professors of the dismal science. And who would say today that people should be rescued from the serfdom of ignorance only in order to make them more productive?'[75]

Education is, to some degree at least, an end in itself. For this reason, not only should more resources be made available for its expansion, but the administration of educational funds should repose in the hands of educators: no outsider, whether from government or from industry, should be allowed to interfere with the academics' autonomy to set priorities and allocate funds as between specific areas of teaching and research. In this way, Galbraith believes, funds will come to be budgeted 'in accordance with humane and intellectual, as opposed to industrial, need'.[76] This might mean that aspiring poets would obtain a greater percentage of educational resources than they do at present; and that, in consequence, aspiring technocrats obtain proportionately less.

Thirdly, educators and other (usually university-trained) intellectuals constitute the principal cultural locus of countervailing power in modern society, a locus growing so rapidly in size and self-awareness that it is actually becoming an independent cause of social change. Galbraith believes, like Marx, that a particular economic order may generate its own gravediggers, and he identifies the educational and scientific estate as the gravediggers of an order orientated towards the needs of the planning system.

The educational and scientific estate is in an exceptionally strong position as, in contemporary industrial societies, 'it holds the critical cards. For in committing itself to technology, planning and organization, the industrial system has made itself deeply dependent on the manpower which these require.'[77] Galbraith believes that the intellectual community has a positive duty both to recognise the power which results from the fact that education is a double-edged sword and to exercise that power in such a way as to challenge the Establishment: 'For the goals that are now important there are no other saviours. In a scientifically exacting world, scientists must assume responsibility for the consequences of science and technology. For custody of the aesthetic dimension of life there is no substitute for the artist.'[78]

Intellectuals are excellently placed to revolt since they occupy key positions in the world of persuasion (as writers, journalists or university teachers, for example), and their power will be multiplied should they in the future be able to form a holy alliance with progressive politicians. Intellectuals have a vested interest in such a revolt, since the emancipation of belief is bound to raise the relative social standing of the professional thinker: 'The intellectual, along with the public official and politician, is the natural competitor of the businessman for what may be called the solemn acclaim of the community.'[79] At present the intellectual enjoys reflected glory, derived from the association of the educator with the training of the prestigious technocracy. A future reorientation of social priorities such as to place greater emphasis on the quality of life rather than the quantity of goods will, however, bestow upon the thinker glory in his own right. The revolt against outdated ideologies has already begun, and for that reason 'the position of the intellectual is now far more secure than that of the businessman'.[80]

Within the intellectual community, the universities have tended to play a particularly significant role. Although vastly expanded principally in order to provide technocrats in response to industrial need, they have paradoxically become havens for critical and vocal dissidents. The academic (unlike those members of the intelligensia who are muzzled by the large organisations by which they are employed) enjoys academic freedom reinforced by security of tenure to prevent dismissal for heresy, and he has not hesitated to utilise that freedom in the social interest by speaking out forcefully and logically against, say, the folly of defence-procurement as a device for underwriting advanced technology, or to make the public aware of manipulative advertising. Just as the academic was once concerned with the emancipation of the body from hunger and disease, so 'nothing in our time is more important'[81] than for him to become involved in the battle for men's minds. And this has happened:

> The universities have become perhaps the most powerful political influence in the United States. It was the universities – not the trade unions, not the free-lance intellectuals, not the Press, not the businessmen, although they helped to a greater degree than is commonly understood – which led the opposition to the Vietnam war, which forced the retirement of President Johnson, which are forcing the pace on the present withdrawal from Vietnam, which are leading the battle against the great corporations on the issue of pollution, and which at the last congressional elections retired a score or more of the more egregious time-servers, military syncophants and hawks.[82]

Some academics, of course, still retain the intellectual's traditional contempt for worldly practice. More and more, however, the academic community has become 'a decisive instrument of political power',[83] aware of the 'obligation imposed by its position in the economic and political structure'[84] and of the fact that ideas have consequences when accompanied by group action. In the 1930s and 1940s, for example, it was the economists at Harvard (led by Alvin Hansen, supported by the central bankers, and operating in the propitious circumstances created by the Great Depression and the New Deal) who were in the vanguard in introducing the Keynesian system to America. Galbraith himself was one of them: 'All of us were committed to a degree of evangelism I've never felt since.

There was an enormous feeling we could change things. In some ways it was a very misleading experience, you had such a sense of what an intellectual could accomplish. From that time on we all believed that if you had the right ideas, nothing stood in your way – it could be done.'[85] Circumstances were then favourable and economists did not fear disquieting innovation. In such a situation, 'what was elaborated in the world of ideas could be destroyed in the world of ideas; what economists gave they could take away.'[86]

Even pure scientists are abandoning passivity in favour of social scrutiny and political involvement, 'especially where science impinges on foreign policy': 'The nuclear test ban treaty of 1963 would not have been achieved except by the initiative of the scientific community. General public and political awareness of the dangers of nuclear conflict, the desirability of *détente* with the Soviet Union and the technical possibilities for disarmament owes a great deal to the scientific community. It owes very little to the military, diplomatic and industrial community.'[87]

Fourthly, educational institutions (and, once again, chiefly the universities) concentrate the young, enlighten them, and channel their instinctive alienation from the Establishment into pressures for social reform. Students come in this way to fight alongside their teachers for an emancipation of belief. After all, dissillusioned with affluence, aware of manipulation, keen to discover more authentic life-styles, students and their contemporaries are already showing considerable anxiety lest they become young fogies:

> The purposes of the system are being questioned in a more specific way by younger people, by many, though not all, of the university generation that the industrial system has itself called into being. They no longer automatically accept its values. They question its working disciplines; the notion that you work hard and competitively five days a week or more to maximise consumption on the other two. Somewhat selectively (more on clothing than electronics) they have come to reject the persuasion which sustains its consumption.[88]

Students are a threat to the 'world of competitive consumption'[89] because of their propensity to adopt non-conformist attitudes towards material values. They are also a threat to the process of disciplined production, since graduates who have been taught the virtues of individuality and critical thought will not find it easy to integrate themselves into the collegiate atmosphere of the techno-structure or to accept purposes not their own. Schools of business are consequently even now losing prestige and reporting a decline in the quality of their applicants: 'Good students, when asked about business, are•increasingly adverse. They hold it to be excessively disciplined, damaging to individuality, not worth the high pay, or dull.'[90] Clearly, whereas the classical proletariat is integrated and passive, the youthful radical is a genuine force for change; for at the very least 'the young have a reassuring tendency to take a fresh view of life'.[91] This is visible even in the State Department: 'One must admire the broad preparation and eclectic outlook of the younger members of our foreign service. Our foreign policy is passing into good hands.'[92] Men who have already invested heavily in in-tellectual capital remain with their obsolete convictions; but the new generation is fresh, sceptical and open.

This is not to say that Galbraith has no reservations concerning the Alternative Society of the youth culture. He is opposed to the taking of drugs and to the reluctance to work on the part of many of the discontented, as also to the use of violence in demonstrations and to student participation in university government:

> I do not believe that a university can be wholly successful unless it reposes strong and responsible power in those who teach, and unless those who teach delegate as needed to their own repre-sentatives. In recent times Latin American universities have been experimenting with highly democratic direction in which stu-dents, graduates, and faculty all participate more or less equally. It is a formula for deterioration into incoherence and chaos. The university is by nature an oligarchy of its faculty.[93]

Such a recommendation might have satisfied 'Old Tommy' (Galbraith's authoritarian schoolmaster in Ontario[94]), but it will hardly appeal to the student activist (to the militant member of 'the bearded and barefoot left'[95]). It is nonetheless totally in keeping with Galbraith's general orientation: just as the logic of the technostructure precludes worker participation, so the health of the university presupposes that power repose firmly in the hands of those best suited to lead.

Fifthly, educators (together, in the nature of things, with their faithful apprentices and disciples, and working in conjunction with intellectuals outside the education industry) not only constitute the crucial force for social reform but also provide a valuable example of an alternative life-style. Culturally as well as politically they thus provide countervailing power, for while on the one hand they do agree to train cadres for industry, on the other they appear to reject the values of the acquisitive society: 'Excessive attention to goods is considered gauche; an elderly automobile or a Volkswagen, casual and shabby clothing, undistinguished but ostentatiously comfortable furniture, self-designed entertainment, unluxurious travel, the absence of a television receiver, and functionally clothed women are sources of distinction.'[96] Intellectuals, as drop-outs from a manipulated way of life, are the first sign of spring after a long, hard winter of dominance by the technostructure; show by their example the proper perspective from which commodity-utility and economic growth should be regarded; and cause the planning system to 'fall into its place as a detached and autonomous arm of the State, but responsive to the larger purposes of the society'.[97]

Educators (like all members of that 'New Class' which aspires to interesting and stimulating employment rather than to maximisation of income) place a premium on job-satisfaction, fulfillment and creativity, and here too they provide a model for others to follow. Even economists whose professional lives are spent drawing upward-sloping supply curves of effort with respect to cash consideration expect to express their personality by means of their work.[98]

Members of the 'New Class' are, of course, well paid; but they also work in clean and comfortable surroundings, exercise their intelligence, and have the opportunity to influence plan and even purpose of their organisation. They are almost without exception free from the 'industrial drudgery' of hard, boring, routine toil, and in this differ from manual labourers: 'The most unfortunate people are those who must do the same thing over and over again, every minute, or perhaps twenty to the minute. They deserve the shortest hours and the highest pay.'[99] Members of the 'New Class', in brief, because they enjoy work as well as play, are the men of the future; and the 'central goal of the society', now that goods are plentiful, must increasingly be to extend to all citizens a similar chance to 'maximise the rewards of all the hours of their days'.[100] This means, on the one hand, automation to replace the need for mere toil, for work *qua* work; and, on the other hand, accelerated recruitment to the 'New Class'. Naturally, once such upgrading has become a major social goal, then 'since education is the operative factor in expanding the class, investment in education, assessed qualitatively as well as quantitatively, becomes very close to being the basic index of social progress'.[101]

Academics within the 'New Class' have long enjoyed a particular benefit, namely a wide range of options and choices with respect to the trade-off between income and leisure; and Galbraith recommends that this benefit be extended to all members of the 'New Class' (to men such as, for example, managers and technocrats, whose work is pleasant but whose hours are prescribed) and, more generally, to all members of society. Such a multiplicity of alternatives could be made available by allowing the employee to select the number of hours he works per day, the number of days per week, the number of weeks per year, for, while Galbraith nowhere calls for legislation to make compulsory a shorter working week, he highly values pluralism, diversity and recognition of the fact that not all families have identical preference-patterns, needs and tastes: 'Few things enlarge the liberty of the individual more substantially than to grant him a measure of control over the amount of his income.'[102] Again, leaves of absence (paid or unpaid) could be offered, possibly to learn something totally unconnected with the employee's usual tasks; and the old could be given the opportunity to retire earlier on respectable pensions, the young the freedom to postpone entry into the labour-force through a substantial extension of their education.

In the on-going struggle between overtime and undertime, academics will probably opt for the latter; for, assigning a relatively low priority to relentless ambition, material goods and money mania, they are unafraid to set themselves target incomes and beyond that point to substitute leisure for potential commodity consumption. Within his peer-group, moreover, an academic who sets himself non-economic goals and displays high leisure-preference is unlikely to be stigmatised as wicked, lazy, shiftless or unpatriotic. The problem with leisure-time interests in the outside community, however, is that at the moment many men do not have any, which possibly explains better than the work-ethic why in recent years the working week has not been falling: because of want-creation, men demonstrably put the boredom of toil before the boredom of rest. The twin problems of lack of interests and commodity-lust must clearly be tackled simultaneously. Fortunately, this can be done by education, which can both make commodities seem as insignificant as they really are and make creative hobbies at least as satisfying as work. Leisure-preference and spiritual fulfillment must be taken very seriously indeed in an affluent society where demand *ex* manipulation is approaching zero, and here as usual educated men are the harbingers of what is to come.

V EVALUATION

Galbraith presents himself as a determinist attempting to identify the cage of circumstance and define the momentum inherent in matter; and states categorically that 'the enemy of the conventional wisdom is not ideas but the march of events'.[103] In fact, however, it is ideas rather than events which ultimately occupy the central place in his perhaps somewhat simplistic model.

All determinism is depressingly fatalistic in nature in so far as it suggests that man's freedom to select *what ought to be* is severely limited by the constraint of *what has to be*; and the pure coincidence that the laws of historical evolution correspond so precisely to Galbraith's own view of social progress is a fortuitous accident so comforting as to be disturbing. Indeed, upon closer inspection the correlation reveals itself to be a spurious one, dependent upon highly questionable assertions (concerning the nature and functioning of the large corporation, the evolution and role of the trade union, the artificiality of consumer tastes and the power of the corporation to mould them as it sees fit, the absence of any alternative to a prices and incomes policy), a selective choice of examples (the 'new socialists' are conspicuously absent from many highly successful private corporations and a major nuisance in many a socialised one) and some mistakes (not all schools of business are reporting a decline in the quality of their applicants, not all businessmen and engineers find their work soul-destroying, not all skilled personnel emerge via the educational bottleneck). Galbraith in short, as might have been expected, has chosen to construct a theory of historical evolution based upon isolated examples and arguments of which many would question the validity, and he compounds his error by neglecting the extent to which inevitability can still take the form of a spectrum of choices rather than indicate a unique solution. Yet, clearly, the economy could be coordinated by more competition as well as by more planning, and Lockheed could be forced to adopt sounder business practices instead of being sheltered under the perpetually outstretched wing of an overprotective public parent. More fundamentally, the present-day abuses of technocrats and bureaucrats might lead to a general recognition that progressive politicians are the natural guardians of the public purpose; but they might also lend to a general revulsion towards other-directedness and State intervention (finding expression, say, in demands for the re-privatisation of State medical, insurance and housing schemes). It would be wrong to exaggerate the extent to which collectivist and étatist tendencies are already well entrenched in an economic and social system nominally anti-interventionist in nature: the market ideology still teaches possessive and individualist rather than cooperative and corporatist values, and its demonstrated inability to explain much of the real world might generate public pressures for a move backward to the simple textbook world of the competitive entrepreneur and the hedonistic consumer rather than a move forward to an even more bureaucratised social order. If bad predictions are at present a negation of scientific economics, there is still no reason to suppose that the market ideology will be discredited and vanquished. It might be revived; for there is no guarantee that all people share the same view of the 'good life' as Professor Galbraith, nor will enthusiastically welcome the 'happy end' which he both predicts and advocates.

Particularly unconvincing is Galbraith's view of the intellectual community as a powerful threat to Establishment practices, a view which from the outset is misleadingly presented in such a way as to disguise its strongly idealist implications. Galbraith regards it as highly significant that the laws of motion of the planning system itself generate a force able to divert that motion and alter those laws; but he underestimates the importance of the fact that intellectuals operate chiefly through the propagation of a countervailing ideology capable of destroying the false and unhealthy ideas propounded by the technostructure and its allies. Yet in so far as intellectuals fight with opinions rather than photographs of reality, they may be said not to emancipate belief so much as to alter it. There is, of course, no reason why a humane value-system should not attack and rout an unpleasant and nasty one; but it must be made clear that the appeal is here at the level of ideas rather than imposed by the march of events. It would perhaps have been more honest had Galbraith abandoned materialism altogether and declared openly, with Keynes, that men are ruled by ideas and by little else.

It is mere quibbling over words to say that intellectuals would never have had the power-base from which to preach progress if the needs of the technostructure had not made them so numerous, not least because not all intellectuals are progressives. Galbraith assumes that scholars 'speak generally for a rational view' and are, like all radicals, 'men of goodwill'.[104] Yet many academics in fact vote conservative and support contemporary ideology and institutions, both economic (many academics despite the affluent society demonstrate exceptional commodity-hedonism and marked hostility to social welfare) and political (many academics opposed the entry of China into the United Nations and supported the intervention in Vietnam as vociferously as the careerists of the State Department). Many academics, moreover, have spent lengthy periods in bureaucracies – public and private – and are dependent on them for research grants (to do research on commercial, industrial or even defence-related problems[105]): this gives them a shared background with organisation-men and a common pecuniary vested interest in the *status quo*. Since ten years work in the Pentagon is unlikely to make a man particularly radical when he emerges, and since it is highly probable that engineers in the universities share the same values as those in private enterprise, it is doubtful that Galbraith has in mind merely economists (the most blatant example, in his view, of academic accommodation to the goals of the planning system) when he confesses that 'a number of very presentable college professors . . . are recruited for their ability to give the Establishment truths a solid doctrinal basis'.[106]

In reality, many academics are uninterested in social questions; and the degree of consensus among those who are enlightened is so low that it would be nonsense to speak of 'estate-consciousness'. Fundamentally, intellectuals are like other people, and may be as gullible, selfish, attached to material possessions, anxious to obtain status-symbols as other men. In India, faced with $15,000 worth of books donated by the Ford Foundation, Galbraith himself made a depressing discovery concerning a substantial section of the academic world:

> I was . . . forced to the conclusion that a great many pieces of scholarly research, as they are called, are published each year that can't be of very much interest even in the United States, for the reason that they are not very intelligent. There was a steady accumulation of books on the shelves, many of them from the

university presses and mostly on history, politics, and social criticism, which were heavy, unimaginative, parochial, dreary, and mechanical rather than thoughtful – though with adequate footnotes and index. I could not bring myself to give these books away. I suppose they did earn the man his promotion.[107]

It is simply not clear why such men should value the countryside or a national health service more highly than material goods, why intellectuals too should not be prisoners of false consciousness in a consumer-orientated society.

Galbraith's optimism appears even less justified when one turns from professors to consider their students. After all, while students do demonstrate in favour of progressive politicians and against recruitment on campus by defence-related industries, they also demonstrate in favour of the material values represented by higher scholarships and better refectories, and many a university teacher has wondered if middle age does not begin at eighteen. Young people are clearly anxious to make money and to spend it; the youth market is without doubt a vast one; and Galbraith's argument that a 'whole generation'[108] is rejecting producer-persuasion is both exaggerated (many boys and girls have yet to grasp the low urgency of consumer-satisfactions in a world of abundance) and incomplete (since his neglect of interdependent preference patterns conceals the vital importance to the status-seeking young of style, emulation and conformity). The youth culture need not be a hopeful portent for the future if it only means high profits for fashion boutiques vending uniforms of flowers to a generation as devoured by cupidity as that of its elders.

Furthermore, many of the young people most alienated from the purposes of the technostructure demand solutions which Galbraith himself would abhor; for it is logical to expect the same individualism that allegedly makes students unwilling to subordinate themselves unquestioningly to the goals of organisation (whether as bureaucrats, soldiers or consumers) also to drive them into the tranquil Haight Ashbury's of the mind or the violent arms of the extreme Left. At the very least, such individualism could make students disruptive of the academic gerontocracy that Galbraith, as we have seen, tends to favour. It is no surprise that Galbraith himself is often resented by his students. The Harvard *Crimson* once wrote of him that 'his course is taught in harangues, followed up by question periods in which hapless students either serve up items to support

Galbraith's theories, or are wittily and thoroughly demolished for failing to do so.'[109] And a former student described his teaching methods as follows to *Time* magazine: 'Vague platitudes on assorted cosmic questions are apparently received through the office of divine revelation.'[110] While one suspects that Galbraith may find the classroom slow and boring after Washington and New York, it is clear that mocking intolerance of other men's self-deception will not appeal to all students and certainly not to the more radical among them. It is curious that Galbraith himself does not show in the classroom that same acceptance of diversity which he elsewhere praises so highly.

In any case, even if professors and students were able to make common cause, and even if the whole intellectual community (inside and outside the universities) were to see itself as the bringer of a particular body of new ideas to a world rich in goods but poor in insights, it still remains doubtful whether thinkers would in fact have much influence save on the literate and articulate sections of the middle classes. Intellectuals have no independent political machine or traditional base in the trade unions or ethnic groups, few have private fortunes, and all are subject to some distrust as eggheads cloistered in ivory towers with revolting students (despite what Galbraith insists is their heightened prestige in a skill-intensive world). If intellectuals are ever to enjoy power, it will hence probably have to be in the wake of politicians; and politicians for their part are unlikely to be as impressed by grandiose theoretical systems as President Kennedy was by *The Affluent Society*.[111]

Perhaps this is just as well, for Galbraith's conception of an intellectual community drawing attention to existing social short-comings and creating a climate of opinion such that a politician who opposes reform will be defeated at the polls is in essence an unacceptably undemocratic one. It could be argued that the power to shape a nation's consciousness should not be placed in the hands of any minority group whatsoever and that Galbraith both underestimates the dangers implicit in the Platonic ideal of philosopher-rulers and the likelihood that the real rulers will (like the technostructure) absorb tame philosophers and thus bombard the electorate with intellectual as well as political arguments in support of a particular ideological orientation.

Galbraith underestimates the menace of manipulated perceptions, and the reason is his avowed determinism. He says that 'most ideas do begin with a relatively small group and spread out from there',[112] but clearly intends this to apply to sensible ideas taking root in the right conditions. His view is that although intellectuals may strike the decisive match, a forest fire only results when the timber is dry, and thus that although a particular élite may act as the vanguard of progress, progress nonetheless has a momentum of its own.

Naturally, if ideas are not the result but the cause of circumstances, then the position of the élite must be reconsidered in the light of its greatly enhanced free will. Where choices are real and not fictitious, then ideology, belief, values and judgements become of the utmost importance.

8 The Vested Interest

Galbraith argues that, in consequence of an out-of-date and unhealthy belief system, 'we do many things that are unnecessary, some that are unwise, and a few that are insane'.[1] He also argues that if we are to defeat that system, we must first identify those groups in modern society which have a vested interest in its propagation, diffusion and perpetuation.

In this chapter we shall examine and evaluate Galbraith's attitude to four groups which he regards as the pillars of contemporary ideology.

I LAZY THINKERS

Belief can be 'a womb in which the individual rests without the pain of mental activity or decision',[2] and some lazy minds find it 'a far, far better thing to have a firm anchor in nonsense than to put out on the troubled seas of thought'.[3] Here the stereotype plays an important role: 'We are less likely to have an understanding of great events than of lesser ones because we are far more massively committed to the wrong view.'[4] Great events (such as the Depression of the 1930s) burn themselves into the popular consciousness and it is hence difficult for the sociologist or the historian to put across a view of things different from that which has already entered the realm of folkore. People cling with frightening obstinacy to what they think they understand: 'It has often been said that every generation rewrites history to its own tastes and specifications. This would appear to be unduly optimistic. Where great events are concerned there is every evidence that the moving finger sticks.'[5]

Men cling 'as though to a raft' to those ideas which 'they have so laboriously learned'[6], and this conservative bias is magnified by the fact that people experience nostalgia for the past as well as attachment to the present. Such nostalgia for earlier social arrangements (say, for the world of the entrepreneur and the small business) reinforces outdated attitudes and ideologies (with respect to, say, the market mechanism and State intervention).

Explanations relating to the past appear temptingly simple because the past itself appears refreshingly uncomplicated when compared with the present. Partly this is because theories have already been developed about past institutions that render them comprehensible; whereas newer phenomena are not yet the subject of familiar theories, and often cannot be studied at all because of the absence of literature that deals with them. Partly too this is because past phenomena are typically idealised and simplified for purposes of textbook presentation, for simplicity is a great aid to understanding.

Confusion is pain to a closed mind, and there is hence a tendency for the lazy thinker to opt for the familiar and the comprehensible even when he knows things have changed: after all, he will reason, the change may not have been permanent and decisive but a mere short-run deviation from a comfortingly well-known trend.

II THE TECHNOSTRUCTURE AND ITS ALLIES

Many organisation men will resent the world of the future which Galbraith envisages. The technostructure has a vested interest in *laissez-faire* (liking his autonomy, the technocrat no more welcomes State directives than guidance from the shareholders) and in the continuing prestige of production (being well aware that the reduced importance of earning and spending heightens the relative power and status of the politician and ultimately compels the technocrat to subordinate himself to the goals of the wider community rather than imposing his own goals at will on the nation). The technostructure, knowing that security and growth would be imperilled should workers have targeted incomes, take unexpected leaves of absence or demand greater job-satisfaction, is pleased that it has been able to forge close links with the working classes (who share its interest in commodity-utility) and the trade union movement (which shares its concern with an expansion of private production in the cause of pay and promotion and who join it in demanding public procurement as an alternative to redundancies while simultaneously opposing public interference with the wage-bargain). And both technostructure and the unions have been able to make common cause with the civil service, particularly in supporting aggressive foreign policy and the Cold War ideology which led to the disaster of Vietnam.[7]

The most one can say of the technostructure is that it is at least a good enemy; for, like the intellectual (and despite specious arguments concerning the link between monetary rewards and incentives), the technocrat is not responsive exclusively to pecuniary motivation. The technocrat is anxious to identify himself with social goals (albeit this is painful where the collective consciousness prescribes deceleration of the growth-rate); and, since all organisation men value standing as well as pay, he may be prepared to channel his expertise away from defence-related programmes and into the fight against poverty (albeit the former probably offers more scope for technological virtuosity that the latter) should public opinion come down unambiguously on the side of reform. Such a man is not a maximum threat to progress, for in the last analysis he will bend with the wind and conform so as not to be left behind.

The technostructure in any case gains as well as loses from a greater degree of State intervention: national planning minimises inconvenient shortages, incomes policy reduces the danger of competitive retaliation, and public support to industry and welfare represents a valuable free gift. Many publicly provided services (ranging from roads to education) are complementary to, not competitive with, private production. The technostructure ought to know that such State activities are not a burden or a drain on private enterprise: it is itself, after all, produced largely in State institutions, and to turn on its creator would be an act of filial disloyalty comparable only to that of Frankenstein's monster. Indeed, the technostructure is probably less opposed than the classical entrepreneur even to reformist schemes (such as social insurance or environmental control) from which the corporation does not itself directly benefit: the cost can be passed backward to the faceless capitalist or forward to the manipulated consumer, and thus, as far as the technocrat is concerned, it is the others who pay.

III THE RICH

The vested interest of the well-to-do is an important reason why politicians (particularly in a world of progressive taxation) are reluctant to put up taxes to pay for an expanded welfare state and similar projects. The fact is that many voters are in search of a

> superior moral justification for selfishness. It is an exercise which always involves a certain number of internal contradictions and even a few absurdities. The conspicuously wealthy turn up urging the character-building value of privation for the poor. The man who has struck it rich in minerals, oil, or other bounties of nature is found explaining the debilitating effect of unearned income from the State. The corporation executive who is a superlative success as an organization man weighs in on the evils of bureaucracy. Federal aid to education is feared by those who live in suburbs that could easily forego this danger, and by people whose children are in private schools. Socialized medicine is condemned by men emerging from Walter Reed Hospital. Social Security is viewed with alarm by those who have the comfortable cushion of an inherited income. Those who are immediately threatened by public efforts to meet their needs – whether widows, small farmers, hospitalized veterans, or the unemployed – are almost always oblivious to their danger.[8]

The rich hence have a vested interest in economic growth. Growth is conducive to full employment, means a buoyant business environment (with a reduced threat of bankruptcies) and makes possible the celebrated truce on inequality; for when the cake is growing conservatives and radicals, historically speaking, cease to squabble over how it is shared out. In general, there appears to be a high correlation in a nation between conservative temperament and personal prosperity, with the implication that 'as the United States proceeds to higher levels of well-being, there is certain to be a steady retreat from social experiment'.[9] As an example of the way in which social experiment is 'severely blighted by prosperity', consider the case of the New Deal: 'It was adversity that nurtured this programme; with prosperity social invention came promptly to an end. . . . In a country where well-being is general, the astute politician will be the one who stalwartly promises to defend the *status quo*.'[10] The implication is that inertia and prudence have a higher income-elasticity than does sympathy with the anguish of the urban ghetto; and that resistance to change and reform is hence on the increase. Pity the poor man who lives in a rich country – other things being equal.

IV THE ECONOMISTS

Neo-classical economists are the ideologues of market capitalism. It is they who implant obsolete ideas concerning choice, allocation and growth in the minds of impressionable students, and whose conventional wisdom, like any other secular theology, is used unscrupulously by Establishment politicians, television commentators and other pundits 'less to reveal truth than to reassure students and other communicants as to the benign tendency of established social arrangements.'[11]

Economists are not corrupt men. They teach the young in a way which, 'rather systematically, excludes speculation on the way the large economic organizations shape social attitudes to their ends', but the service is rendered, 'in the main, in innocence and in the name of scientific truth'.[12] Indeed, were the service arranged and paid for, 'it would cease to be of much effect'.[13] Simply, economists have a vested interest in textbook economics (which they spent many long years learning) and in economic goals and values (as they would otherwise presumably not be economists), and 'the greatest of vested interests' are 'those of the mind'.[14] Economists, 'like other people, have an instinct for what is worthy, responsible and reputable'[15], and even if they did not believe their own propaganda, personal advancement in their profession depends on adherence to its values.

Quite simply, 'a reputation for soundness in our day continues to rest on a zealous avoidance of novelty, while no one is so admired for his wisdom as the man who reacts sympathetically to change and then explains why it is unwise'.[16] As a result, economists (like civil servants) very often prefer the comfortable and the accepted to the disturbing and the original. In such a situation, 'the bland lead the bland'[17] without the resulting instrumental function of neo-classical economics being *prima facie* evidence for a conspiracy theory of history. Economists do make a living from 'the infinitely interesting gadgetry of disguise',[18] but they are seldom *deliberately* subservient to the ideological needs of the giant organisation.

The fact remains that textbook economics does have an ideological function, and the reason here is that it has lost touch with present-day conditions. Galbraith stresses that the orthodox picture 'is not implausible as a description of a society that once existed'[19] (and that still exists in the market system), but that it is irrelevant to the conditions that now obtain in the planning system and the State sector. The 'problem of economics', in short, 'is not one of original error but of obsolescence.'[20]

Orthodox economics, precisely *because* it is outdated as a description of contemporary reality, 'performs an instrumental service in guiding attention away from inconvenient fact and action'[21], for 'it happens that the image of an earlier economic society serves admirably the instrumental purposes of a later one'.[22] The ideological function of orthodox economics will become clear once we have considered four examples of the way in which it is today not so much a science as 'a conservatively useful system of belief'.[23]

First, there is the problem of production. Economic ideas are 'the product of a world in which poverty had always been man's normal lot',[24] and thus are 'rooted in the poverty, inequality, and economic peril of the past'.[25] As a consequence, 'we are guided, in part, by ideas that are relevant to another world';[26] for clearly no sensible man 'would wish to argue that the ideas which interpreted this world of grim scarcity would serve equally well for the contemporary United States'.[27]

In the Ricardian world, even necessities like food, clothing, housing and heating were scarce. In the contemporary affluent societies of Western Europe and North America, however, 'goods are abundant. Although there is malnutrition, more die in the United States of too much food than of too little. . . . No one can seriously suggest that the steel which comprises the extra four or five feet of purely decorative distance on our cars is of prime urgency. For many women and some men clothing has ceased to be related to protection from exposure and has become, like plumage, almost exclusively erotic. Yet production remains central to our thoughts.'[28] Economists, by transposing the preoccupations of a poverty-stricken world to a world of abundance, continue to propagate an outdated view of economic growth as the supreme index of social achievement, and in this way unwittingly serve the interests both of large organisations (which are endowed with a prestigious *raison d'être*) and of their own peer-group (since the standing of the economist is related to the urgency of commodity-consumption).

Second, there is the matter of the market. Galbraith argues that economists make the mistake of 'trying to place all problems within the framework of the market and all behaviour subordinate to market command'.[29] Such a fossilised approach to production and allocation quite understandably had valuable prescriptive properties in the context of the world in which economics was born and grew up: 'In a world that had for so long been so poor nothing was so important as to win an increase in wealth. The prescription – to free men from the restraints and protection of feudal and mercantilist society and put them on their own – was sound, for it was already proving itself.'[30] Such an approach, however, is inadequately descriptive of present-day reality; for whereas market freedom was emerging in the eighteenth century, it is in the twentieth being eclipsed.

Once upon a time the consumer was sovereign, the firm small, the entrepreneur a profit-maximiser, the market perfectly competitive; and, by continuing to teach in terms of this pre-corporate ideal, textbook economics has 'slipped imperceptibly into its role as the cloak over corporate power. No one managed the process.'[31] Textbook economics masks the reality of producer power, consumer manipulation, shareholder disenfranchisement, bureaucratic symbiosis and continues to pretend that the giant corporation is no more than the servant of the individual and his authentic choices. Textbook economics, in other words, has the function of mystification, in so far as it 'persuades people that the goals of organization are really their own or paves the way for such persuasion'[32] and serves 'to divert attention from questions of great social urgency which, in the established view, had alarming implications for political action'.[33] Men see what they expect to see, and the neglect of power in economic theories (the assumption that even the modern corporation is 'the nearly powerless automaton of the market'[34]) causes the citizen to fail to notice the reality of power in the world around him. That failure is due not to 'retarded intelligence' but to the 'convenient illusion'[35] of economystic disguise: 'The victims of that disguise are those we instruct in error. The beneficiaries are the institutions whose power we so disguise. Let there be no question: Economics, so long as it is thus taught, becomes, however unconsciously, a part of an arrangement by which the citizen or student is kept from seeing how he is, or will be, governed.'[36]

Third, there is the question of quantification. Economists increasingly present their arguments with an awe-inspiring degree of theoretical sophistication and mathematical refinement. They thus tend to sow confusion among laymen and the uninitiated by a massive flight into the 'wholly incomprehensible'[37], and the trip is not really necessary: 'There are few, if any, useful ideas in economics that cannot be expressed in clear English. Obscurity rarely if ever denotes complexity of subject matter; it never denotes superior scholarship. It usually signifies either inability to write clear English or – and more commonly – muddled or incomplete thought.'[38] A certain degree of obscurity is nonetheless vital if an economist is to make his name in today's world: even Keynes would have been less influential had his *General Theory* not included so many complex concepts and elaborate explanations.[39] Yet 'it would be a mistake to identify complexity with completeness and sophistication with wisdom'.[40] And in any case 'what is wholly mysterious in economics is not likely to be important'.[41]

Partly economists place a premium on rigour and precision in the formulation of arguments because of their concern with outdated ends (notably a rising GNP) and outdated means (notably the market mechanism): accuracy is understandably highly valued where the teleology of a subject is maximisation of efficiency in conditions of scarcity. Yet the vast apparatus of quantification, by excluding the qualitative and the cultural, tends to give an incomplete and biased picture of reality. Numerous important variables cannot be measured but should not be ignored: 'To many it will always seem better to have measurable progress toward the wrong goals than unmeasurable and hence uncertain progress toward the right ones. . . . The questions that are beyond the reach of economists – the beauty, dignity, pleasure and durability of life – may be inconvenient but they are important.'[42] Here again, of course, the orientation of the economists coincides with that of the technostructure inasmuch as both groups are more experienced in dealing with the measurable than with the impressionistic. As far as the economist is concerned, however, the orientation is imposed purely by his loudly trumpeted assertion that the discipline must be kept value-free: 'Reference to the quality of life will be thought replete with value-judgements.'[43] The coincidence of outlook thence inevitably follows: 'The condemnation of value judgements . . . is one of the devices by which scientific pretension enforces adherence to traditional preoccupations.'[44]

Partly, too, economists place a premium on rigour and precision because of their awareness that esoteric jargon and manipulation of symbols raises the prestige of their subject. Indeed, since economists wish to regard themselves as scientists on a par with physicists or chemists, they even tend to argue as if their fundamental theoretical laws were as immutable as the law of gravity:

This explains, in turn, the considerable scientific selfrighteousness with which sophisticated scholars avow the irrelevance of, say, the advent of modern advertising for the theory of demand. It is a libel on the scientific integrity of economics to suppose that its scientific verities are affected by such superficial change. Moreover, the first steps to bring institutional changes within the framework of economic analysis are invariably tentative, oral rather than mathematical and lacking the elegance of a methodological innovation. Hence they are readily dismissed by the men of scientific reputation or pretension as being rather sloppy.[45]

It is true that a more qualitative and less quantitative approach to economics may mean more imprecision. Paradoxically, however, it may also mean an improved likeness of reality: 'There will be fear that once we abandon present theory, with its intellectually demanding refinement and its increasing instinct for measurement, we shall lose the filter by which scholars are separated from charlatans and windbags. These latter are always a danger, but there is more danger in remaining with a world that is not real.'[46]

Fourth, there is the indifference to interdisciplinarity. The problem with economics (and the reason why it today performs an instrumental function in the service of *status quo*) is not simply uncorrected intellectual obsolescence joined to excessive reliance on spurious quantification. The problem is also that overspecialisation which results when one postulates the existence of a separate sector called the economy and attempts to study it in isolation, for 'the world to its discredit does not divide neatly along the lines that separate the specialists'.[47]

It is to the credit of earlier scholars (such as, for example, Smith, Malthus, Bentham and Marx) that they built systems and integrated disciplines now distinct. Compared with the contemporary approach, the earlier synthetic method appears 'less precise but more grand'[48]: 'Here, it seems to me, lies the weakness and even the danger of the current discussion of economic development. We have been enthusiastically and quite capably discussing the parts of the problem; we have paused all too infrequently to inquire whether the parts fit into a viable whole.'[49]

Galbraith emphasises that 'the boundaries of a subject matter are conventional and artificial', and warns that 'none should use them as an excuse for excluding the important'.[50] He notes that a study of the economy is simultaneously a study of society and polity, and expresses his regret that the economist is not professionally equipped to take social and political variables into account: interdisciplinary studies are neglected since the very existence of a separate discipline called economics shows that some men prefer the study of a small sector to a (possibly less rigorous) contemplation of a wider canvas, and since an economist whose work borders too closely on sociology or other disciplines tends to be ranked low in the professional prestige-hierarchy. In this way the economist plays into the hands of the technocrat, who is eager for the economy to be studied in isolation and who in particular welcomes the divorce between economics and politics. It is this separation which Galbraith most virulently attacks. Power and its distribution having become the strategic variables in economy as well as polity, he argues, an integration of economic with political theory is desperately needed:

> Power being so comprehensively deployed in a very large part of the total economy, there can no longer, except for reasons of game-playing or more deliberate intellectual evasion, be any separation by economists between economics and politics. When the modern corporation acquires power over markets, power in the community, power over the state, power over belief, it is a political instrument, different in form and degree but not in kind from the state itself. To hold otherwise – to deny the political character of the modern corporation – is not merely to avoid the reality. It is to disguise the reality.[51]

Interdisciplinary studies are a threat to the position of the technostructure in so far as they demonstrate the subordination of the majority to the power of a minority rather than to the market. They are also a threat to economics itself in so far as economics could 'become like sociology and partly a branch of political theory'.[52] This economists will resist since the instinct for self-preservation tells them that their own importance and prestige (like that of the technostructure) is related to the importance and prestige of goods and services. Thus, 'allowing for numerous exceptions, they will be prone to identify economic goals with all of life. They are not, accordingly, the best proponents of the public, aesthetic and intellectual priorities on which the quality and safety of life increasingly depend'.[53]

Economists are, in short, the 'natural allies'[54] of the planning system, preaching a gospel of free markets and consumer sovereignty which has the reactionary function of focusing popular attention on 'the familiar, the settled, and the safe'[55]: 'In a world where affluence is rendering the old ideas obsolete, it will continue to be the bastion against the misery of new ones.'[56] Fortunately, the tide is turning. Clearly, 'even economists must agree with a social goal which accords the individual the opportunity of providing for all of his needs, not merely for a part of them.'[57] Economists, particularly younger economists and those integrated in the academic community, have already demonstrated their willingness, in a rich society, to opt for beauty, leisure, slum clearance, cultural pluralism and the absolute value of a humanistic education in preference to the traditional economic goals of growth, employment, and allocative efficiency. Galbraith, today at least, is evidently not alone in believing 'that modern economic life is seen much more clearly when . . . there is effort to see it whole'.[58]

V EVALUATION

Galbraith's theory of those social groupings which have a vested interest in the perpetuation of an outdated ideology is debatable (perhaps because it underestimates the hostility of the technostructure to any interference with business autonomy such as that represented by prices and incomes policy, and because it ignores the support likely to be lent to such resistance by managers, shareholders, residual entrepreneurs and those 'men of goodwill' who do not share Galbraith's views concerning American socialism) and particularly controversial where it treats as having a vested interest in error those social groupings which advance proposals different from Galbraith's own (proposals involving job-sharing as an alternative to involuntary unemployment in a model which seems to foresee displacement of labour in both market and planning systems; proposals involving an extension of self-help and cooperative schemes or a reduction of the role played in social life by rationalisation and bureaucratisation at the cost of spontaneity and conviviality in a model where small can easily become beautiful once there has ceased to be an economic need for large scale and technological revolution; proposals involving employee participation in decision-making, worker-shareholders, alternative technology and widespread deprofessionalisation). More generally,

Galbraith, because of his deterministic adherence to the 'end of ideology' approach and his marked sympathy with the convergence thesis, is weak on alternative scenarios for the future and tends to assume that the Britain of tomorrow will be similar to the America of today; whereas in fact there may be more than one growth-path in an advanced industrial society (as the Soviets, of whose peaceful intentions Galbraith is convinced but which in truth are known only to their present and future leaders, would be the first to point out). And then there is the problem of the fraternity of economists who, unhappy to be cast as the capitalists opposite the intellectuals' classical proletariat in the ideational two-class struggle of the Galbraithian system, will no doubt be anxious to make the following criticisms as economists of the urbane iconoclast and his orientation:

First, Galbraith successfully gives the impression that 'the intellectual capital of the economist is extensively invested in the market'[59]; and that, while the orthodox economist, the victim of myopia and mystification, is still thinking in terms of the small perfect competitor, he, Galbraith, has discovered the existence and significance of the large corporation, advertising, social imbalance, cost-push inflation. Economists will reply, however, that Galbraith is overstating the novelty and originality of his own contribution. Positive economics is concerned with *what is*; and for that reason many scholars have already developed theories of oligopoly (such as E. H. Chamberlain and Joan Robinson, although Galbraith decided as early as 1948 that they only 'substituted a new set of frustrations for the old ones'[60]), absentee ownership (such as J. Burnham, A. Berle and G. Means, or R. Marris), technological progress (such as J. Schumpeter), secular stagnation (such as A. Hansen). All of Galbraith's ideas are not new, and his debt in particular to British Fabianism (notably R. H. Tawney, to whose *The Acquisitive Society* he pays tribute in the title of his most famous work) and American Institutionalism (notably Thorstein Veblen, whose *The Theory of the Leisure Class* is a sophisticated approach to interdependent preference-patterns and whose *The Engineers and the Price System* demonstrates that, with respect to the technostructure, Galbraith was not the first to establish bridgeheads in existing belief[61]) could perhaps be better acknowledged. More generally, Galbraith benefited from having as his colleagues at Harvard some of the most stimulating thinkers of his time, including David Riesman (whose *The Lonely Crowd* remains the classic study of other-directedness),

Daniel Bell (whose work on *The End of Ideology* and *The Coming of Post-Industrial Society* shows concerns paralleling Galbraith's own), Wassily Leontief (the father of input–output analysis and a man with a powerful systemic, structural bias) and Talcott Parsons (the Grand Theoretician and proponent of holistic, functionalist models in which everything depends on everything else). More generally still, many of Galbraith's themes had been anticipated by the popularisations of Vance Packard (notably in *The Hidden Persuaders*) and the polemics of Friedrich von Hayek (notably in *The Road to Serfdom*), as indeed by Peter Drucker in books such as *The Concept of the Corporation*. Galbraith, in short, is neither the first nor the only; and, because he puts forward as novel propositions which have long been accepted as commonplace, he may justly be criticised for giving the middle-brow layman an exaggerated view of his own importance. Still, academic controversy by its very nature means absorption of ideas from others; and, as Galbraith observed after noting how many tourists had carved their name on the Great Wall of China (some Albanian visitors appear to have brought along a chisel expressly for this purpose), one is 'struck by how hard it is to be a pioneer anywhere today'.[62]

Professional economists are unlikely to be fond of Galbraith's caricature of their attitudes as naïve, irresponsible, superficial and out-of-date – as in passages such as the following: 'Economists are economical, among other things, of ideas. It is still so. They make those they acquire as graduate students do for a life-time. Change in economics comes only with the changing generations.'[63] Economists are likely to deny that cost-push inflation is really a phenomenon 'always more visible in fact than in the textbooks'[64] and, no less virulently, that 'although the large corporation, like the union, is far from new, it has never been really assimilated into the main body of economics'.[65] Economists are likely to insist that Galbraith over-stresses the importance of the conventional wisdom of perfect competition and consumer sovereignty in contemporary economics, and thus deliberately chooses to take pot-shots at straw men. To some extent, after all, these constructs are mere expositional devices in what Scott Gordon calls 'the Arcadian world of the elementary text book'.[66] At the same time, however, Galbraith is probably right to say that people expect from a textbook 'what is commonly believed or what is commonly believed to believed',[67] and to stress that most students do not go on to do more advanced courses. Clearly, oversimplification at first-year level can influence a man's ideological framework for life, and for that reason the elementary textbook may truly have a latent function (intellectual support for existing social and economic institutions through an emphasis on the benign nature of market forces and the civilising mission of business activity) quite independent of its manifest function (a gentle introduction to a complex and difficult subject).

Second, Galbraith's work is likely to be regarded as unhelpful by many members of the economics profession because of the breadth of his concerns. Fundamentally, as Solow has put it, Galbraith is a Big Thinker, and yet 'economists are determined little-thinkers. They want to know what will happen to the production of houses and automobiles . . . if Congress votes a 10 per cent surcharge on personal and corporate tax bills, and what will happen if Congress does not. They would like to be able to predict the course of the Wholesale Price Index and its components, and the total of corporate profits by industry. They are not likely to be much helped or hindered in these activities by Professor Galbraith's view of Whither We are Trending.'[68] Solow, however, goes on to describe Galbraith's writings as a useful corrective to an excessively microscopic approach: 'Professor Galbraith makes an eloquent case for big-thinking, and he has a point. Little-thinking can easily degenerate into mini-thinking or even into hardly thinking at all. Even if it does not, too single-minded a focus on how the parts of the machine work may lead to a careful failure ever to ask whether the machine itself is pointed in the right direction.'[69]

The real point is simply this: Galbraith is best understood when regarded neither as a serious economist nor as what Paul Samuelson has called a 'non-economist's economist',[70] but rather as an economic sociologist and a social philosopher. As an economic sociologist with a strongly organicist and systemic bias, Galbraith has attempted to integrate economy with society, polity and culture into a comprehensive whole, and to study problems with which the economist *qua* economist has traditionally not been concerned (problems such as the position of women, interlocking interest-groups, power in organisations, the circulation of élites, the dynamics of political action). As a social philosopher with an eye to the future, Galbraith has sought not so much to found a school as to associate himself with the on-going body of moderate opposition to liberal utilitarianism. Because of his obsession with Whither We are Trending, Galbraith's attack on textbook economics must be recognised for what it is—an important plank in a normative, pro-

Statist political platform. For textbook theories of the market mechanism are in practice an important part of an alternative social philosophy supported not simply by dodo economists but by a very large number of concerned citizens who sincerely believe in the moral supremacy over State intervention and collective consumption of business competition, financial incentives, *laissez-faire*, exchange of equivalents, individual freedom, individual responsibility. It is this alternative ideology which Galbraith is seeking to combat with his model of manipulated man confronting impersonal organisations; with his somewhat artificial dichotomies (where, as Christopher Bliss has pointed out, the reader is faced with a choice between 'on the one hand some naïve and manifestly inadequate viewpoint, on the other Galbraith's own ideas'[71]); with his selective assumptions and sweeping generalisations which acquire the force of evidence; with his spurious economic and technological determinism which converts the moral philosophy of his opponents (with whose arguments he never really comes to grips, and which are perhaps most clearly expounded in Milton Friedman's book *Capitalism and Freedom*) into misguided utopian daydreaming.

The 'conventional wisdom' which serves as Galbraith's target cannot be compared with the 'classical economics' towards which Keynes directed his criticism, for whereas the attack on early macroeconomics focused primarily on the analysis of *what is*, the attack on market capitalism encroaches in addition upon *what ought to be*. Galbraith's attack on textbook economics is based in the first instance on the conviction that it mirrors a view of the world not only out of date and irrelevant but, perhaps more significantly, undesirable and unhealthy as well. It is not in essence the attack of an economist seeking to purify his subject but that of a social critic seeking to transform his society. Galbraith is, of course, entitled to his world-view, and many will no doubt share it; but the unsuspecting reader should nonetheless be alerted to the fact that where there is special pleading there is special danger.

Third, economists are likely to criticise Galbraith for underestimating the utility to society of precise technical apparatus which 'determined little-thinkers' have constructed, and which in truth is a complement to, not a substitute for, Galbraith's own brand of Big Thinking. The efficient use of inputs, after all, is not incompatible with increased leisure-time or an expanded Welfare State, and the construction of quantitative decision-making criteria and the calculation of success-indicators in the public sector can be helpful even when where choices are ultimately not made on economic grounds alone (witness, for example, the value of cost-benefit analysis to the economics of education or slum clearance, as indeed the contribution of orthodox economics to an understanding of public goods, pollution and the incidence of taxation). Galbraith exaggerates the extent to which rigour of presentation has become to economists an end in itself (although some quite celebrated cases could naturally be cited which do support his point) rather than merely a valuable tool used to guard against careless thinking, and he is being most unfair when he dismisses those branches of economics which he personally finds unintelligible (he gives the example of advanced growth models) as incomprehensible in themselves.

The fact is that Galbraith's own arguments would in some cases benefit from the careful restatement and in-depth testing of hypotheses which characterise the approach of the orthodox economist, for ranging widely does not preclude probing deeply. It is, to be fair, not simply the instinct for professional self-preservation that causes the economist to recoil before sentences which begin 'Everyone who wins a positive score in an intelligence test recognizes . . . ',[72] or arguments such as the following: 'A moment's thought . . . will suggest that the present analysis is not in conflict with common observation and common sense.'[73] Nor is it simply professional jealousy that causes the economist to view with suspicion Galbraith's tendency to move without warning from fact to interpretation to value-judgement to cure; to make deduction appear induction by mustering a body of evidence in support of a proposition which itself only makes sense if one accepts some highly questionable prior axiom (such as the replacement of consumer by producer sovereignty); and to blind the reader by the use of dazzling rhetoric to lacunae in the argument (which, should the economist draw attention to them, Galbraith turns to his own advantage by blaming discomfort on a blinkered ideology or a vested interest in error). Economists will acknowledge that Galbraith's works are far more accessible in terms of prose and style than is the case with many economic tracts, but will nonetheless warn against confusing heat with light and will stress the applicability to Galbraith himself of that which he has to say about Veblen: 'It is hard to divorce Veblen's language from the ideas it conveys. The ideas are pungent, incisive and insulting. But the writing itself is also a weapon.'[74] Economists will argue that that weapon can be a dangerous one, and will know that when it comes to polemic they are no match for a man who for five years (1943–8) was on the board of editors of *Fortune* magazine and who has an amazing ability to use words and phrases (not all of them original, as the reader of Smith, Wilde, Tawney, Churchill or even Arthur Schlesinger Jr. will appreciate): Harry Johnson has remarked that 'Professor Galbraith's phrase is his fortune',[75] and it is certainly impressive how expressions like 'countervailing power', 'conventional wisdom' and 'affluent society' have already established themselves in the public domain (with 'technostructure', 'Principle of Consistency' and 'educational and scientific estate' likely soon to follow). Certain economists have even gone so far as to deplore the fact that a man with so little technical apparatus at his command should have been given, in the United Kingdom, two prime opportunities to expound his personal view of market capitalism on the BBC, in the prestigious Reith Lectures (1966) and the thirteen-part series *The Age of Uncertainty* (1977); and have warned that Galbraith's bias might not be recognised by the non-specialist viewer, who might expect a different mix of factual knowledge and political argument from the distinguished Paul M. Warburg, Professor of Economics at Harvard, than he is in fact being offered.

Galbraith's direct contribution to economics is a modest one (and probably confined to his pioneering attempt to develop a theoretical framework for price controls in work done before he became a celebrity in his own right with the publication of his first best-seller in 1952 when he was already forty-four). His indirect contribution, on the other hand, is enormous. He has acted as a catalyst to spark off valuable controversy and discussion among economists concerning social systems and political structures to which many had previously paid too little attention; stimulated economists to think in terms of reform and change as well as costs and benefits (for 'hideous noises', 'raucous laughter' and 'a delicately thumbed nose', while evidently not useful criteria for the Coal Board or the Electricity Council, were nonetheless powerful instruments of intervention when it came to ending the war in Vietnam); and drawn attention to a number of important issues (the quality of life, consumer manipulation, the role of the GNP as an index of social progress, public poverty amidst private affluence, the nature of bureaucracies, the problem of power) that were not commonplace or hackneyed when he first began to write about them. If they have today become familiar topics of conversation and research, it must be at least in part thanks to him. Galbraith's books are among the most important and controversial social critiques to emerge in the troubled quarter-century from Korea to Vietnam, and it is impossible to discuss contemporary political, social and economic issues without having considered the questions he raises and the answers he provides.

9 Conclusion: Galbraith and the Emancipation of Belief

Galbraith is not a prophet of doom. Rather, he is an optimist convinced that the future will be better than the past and that the radical social critic such as himself will help to make it so. The social critic notices a flaw in the existing fabric of society, brings it to the attention of the community, stimulates redress of grievances by provoking political controversy, and thus performs the essential function of mobilising public opinion on the side of progress.

Criticism is the means by which a society acquires free will and is thus 'the engine of change'[1] in all open societies. Beware the collectivity that does not loudly debate its weaknesses: 'The society that does not have a similar need to publicize its shortcomings may be thought by superficial men to have no shortcomings. In fact, it may merely be leaving them uncorrected.'[2]

The emancipation of belief waits on social criticism; and Galbraith, recognising that three key groups of critics are progressive politicians, reformist intellectuals and unorthodox economists, has managed to have a foot in all three camps.

(a) Progressive politicians

Galbraith has never himself actually held an important political post (having resisted the temptation to stand as Governor or Senator in Massachusetts or Vermont), but he has nonetheless consistently been active in the radical wing of the Democratic Party. Thus he was on the campaign staff of Adlai Stevenson in the 1952 and 1956 elections, was close to John Kennedy, seconded the nomination of Eugene McCarthy at the Democratic Convention in Chicago, and offered considerable support to George McGovern in

1972. He was National Chairman of the Americans for Democratic Action from 1967 to 1969.

Galbraith's relationship with President Kennedy is of particular interest. He had known the family for some time, having tutored the brothers at Harvard, and as early as 1958 (the same year as *The Affluent Society* was on the best-seller lists, two years after Stevenson's second defeat and at a time when few Democrats looked to Kennedy) was already introducing the young Senator to influential academics in the Boston area. Galbraith was thus not just a valuable but an early supporter: 'As late as 1959 *Esquire* polled one hundred professors throughout the country about their choice for the Presidency. There were only two votes for Kennedy. One was Galbraith's, and the other that of Crane Brinton, the Harvard historian, who said (to Galbraith's considerable surprise) that he favored Kennedy because the candidate appeared to be a disciple of Galbraith's economics. Kennedy immediately wrote Galbraith, thanking him for preventing a shutout.'[3] Galbraith canvassed widely for Kennedy in the 1960 election (important not only because of Galbraith's personal fame and because the Harvard name accorded added status and authority but also because Galbraith was, after all, a Scottish Protestant supporting an Irish Catholic), wrote speeches for Kennedy to deliver (as he had previously done for Stevenson) and is the author of probably the most famous phrase in Kennedy's inaugural address – 'Let us never negotiate out of fear. But let us never fear to negotiate.'[4] In return, he was able to bask in and share the Kennedy charisma and the glamour of Camelot, to circumvent the bureaucracy and communicate directly with the leader (as when he personally advised Kennedy in 1962 against American involvement in Vietnam) and to demonstrate his own political acumen (notably, when, as American Ambassador in India, he dealt successfully with both the Indian occupation of Goa and the Indo-Chinese border dispute, and also managed to reduce the role played by the CIA in the subcontinent).

(b) Reformist intellectuals

Galbraith believes that intellectuals such as himself, by influencing public opinion, help to alter the attitudes of incumbent politicians and also help to create a climate in which true progressives (men who can without difficulty distinguish 'the public interest from the corporate interest, the popular interest from the privileged interest'[5]) will be elected. Such a man was George McGovern, who in 1972 explicitly spelled out his position on welfare, the military and tax reform with admirable frankness: 'Only an honest and serious man bothers to tell you exactly what he hopes to do, and these qualities evidently appeal to voters these days.'[6] McGovern could afford to be honest, for he believed himself to be advocating 'the kind of change that most voters want'.[7] His policies, Galbraith prophesied, 'will be far from bad at the polls'[8]: 'He will appeal to the unrich, unpowerful, and unprivileged majority, and, therefore, like Roosevelt, he will be elected.'[9] History records that Galbraith's optimistic prediction was unjustified in so far as McGovern (like Stevenson and McCarthy) was not elected, but also that Galbraith was able to draw comfort even from failure: 'This defeat needs to be appraised in light of the newness of the effort. No candidate disposed to such general support of public purposes or such criticism of the purposes of the planning system had ever come close to nomination.'[10] The defeat meant to Galbraith no more than this: progressive politicians will only be elected by a progressive electorate, by an electorate that has been made progressive by the reasoned arguments to which it has been exposed, and the case of McGovern at least testifies to a growing public awareness of the divergence between social and corporate purpose. It is ironical that while the very next election did indeed see the victory of the Democrats, the candidate in 1976 was Jimmy Carter, a man who was in no way noticeably in debt to Galbraith's economic and social ideas and who in his campaign quietly but firmly turned down Galbraith's offer of assistance.

At the same time, it would be wrong to imply that Galbraith has been unsuccessful in his efforts to influence public opinion, or to underestimate the impact of his work on American society in the 1950s, 1960s and 1970s. Two contributions in particular might be cited which suggest (at least to Galbraith himself) that reformist intellectuals have consequences.

First, the years immediately following the appearance of *The Affluent Society* saw an extension of activity in the United States in the social welfare field, and *post hoc* was probably *propter hoc*, as Galbraith made clear in a radio interview in 1965:

I think we have become somewhat more aware of the importance of maintaining a balance between our private wealth and our public services, which was the main point that I made. Many of the enlarged public efforts in the last few years in the field of urban redevelopment, urban planning, particularly in education and the alleviation of privation – these things owe at least a little to the discussion that followed the book. An author is not likely, as you know, to minimize his importance, and I've never been accused of doing it.[11]

Second, the withdrawal from Vietnam is to be explained not principally in terms of dramatic gestures of protest (such as marches, pickets, demonstrations or campus boycotts on military recruitment and defence-related research projects) but more fundamentally in terms of the power of public opinion and the pressure of national consensus on the President: 'We have in President Johnson an admirably sensitive political leader. He can be counted on to see where greatness lies.'[12] Since public opinion and national consensus are variables and not constants, however, the power of the reformist intellectual is great; and Galbraith (not least through his pamphlet *How To Get Out of Vietnam*, which sold 250,000 copies in 1967) seized every opportunity to affect the mood of the country. Reasoned argument widely disseminated, he believed, would be more effective in the long-run than noisy demonstrations in the streets:

> I have always been associated with that opposition to the war which is strictly legal, which indeed has a very large measure of decorum. I have felt that the most important thing was to persuade the middle-class business and professional people whose commitment is very strongly to the framework of law . . . There are many different ways in which people can express themselves on the war. My instinct is to express myself within the framework of the political process. I haven't marched; I don't carry signs.[13]

(c) Unorthodox economists

Galbraith's writings are much criticised by his peers for being journalistic and superficial rather than scholarly and profound. A typical comment is that of *The Economist*: 'The habitual reader of economic textbooks has a vested interest in hoping that he can get more sustenance from this champagne than from his usual diet of dog biscuits. But, after reading the author's famous preliminary canter in *The Affluent Society*, one is still left heretically doubting how much really lies behind the bubbly.'[14] The reply here, however, is that Galbraith for two decades regarded himself as virtually isolated within the economics profession; that he believed himself forced in consequence to aim at a much wider readership than that of specialists alone; and that he fully appreciated how essential simplification and verbal brilliance are likely to prove if one seeks to reach a generalist audience. For a generalist audience has clearly been his target, as David Halberstam reported shortly after the publication of *The New Industrial State*: 'Galbraith looks upon the success of his latest book as entirely predictable. He believes that there are 100,000 to 200,000 quite serious Americans who are perplexed about what is going on in the industrial state and who find the average monograph too technical and narrow for their taste, and the average popularization too light. He was deliberately shooting for this middle ground.'[15]

To some extent, Galbraith would argue, this appeal to a generalist audience was not so much chosen as thrust upon him by the refusal of orthodox economists to take his ideas and proposals seriously. Economists paid little attention to his early and somewhat demanding treatise *A Theory of Price Control* (1952), of which he says that it was 'the best book I ever wrote in many ways. It was a tough technical essay and maybe fifty people read it and it had absolutely zero influence. I made up my mind then that I was not going to invest any more of my time that way. From now on I would put in an extra year on the writing to engage a larger audience, and because of that the other economists would have to react to me. My work would not be ignored.'[16] By engaging a wider readership, in other words, Galbraith was not merely seeking to provoke the general public to question their assumptions (although admittedly he does believe that 'no economist ever had the slightest influence who wrote only for economists'[17]), but to force unpopular truths on the economics profession by means of the back door precisely because he regarded the front door as securely locked and bolted. To some extent he has succeeded: not only has he aroused much interest among younger economists (and among vast numbers of his peers, since he was elected President of the American Economic Association for 1971–2), but his criticisms (particularly since the appearance of *The New Industrial State* in 1967) have increasingly figured prominently in the new textbook economics. This tendency must be a source of great satisfaction to him, since he has written as follows concerning the central role of education in the process of social liberation: 'The place where understanding should begin is where economics is taught. People of compulsive anxiety, conservatives in particular, have recurrent spasms over the books that are being used in the universities. Their instinct is, I think, sound. Only as ideas work their way into the matrix of university instruction do they become really influential.'[18]

Galbraith believes that ideas are contagious, and that public opinion at large can be influenced and must be mobilised. Following the assassination of President Kennedy (and at a time when the act was still widely believed to be the work of right-wing extremists), Galbraith's first thoughts were not of disturbed individuals and sick minds but of the disturbed and sick society that could produce such a tragedy: 'My strongest thought was that we were paying the price for the poisonous hatred stirred up so casually by the extreme right. Somehow or other, national indignation should have intervened to shut them up and thus to have excluded the incitement to violence for those whose mental discrimination is too slight.'[19] And at a ceremony at the Capitol the day before the funeral, Galbraith once again reflected on how much human ideas are social facts: 'The Chief Justice gave a magnificent talk and he said the one thing that needed to be said, namely that while few will advocate assassination, many will contribute to the climate which causes men to contemplate it.'[20]

If many can contribute to a sick social climate, then many can contribute to a healthy one. Galbraith believes that the social critic, whether as progressive politician, reformist intellectual or unorthodox economist, has a positive obligation to persuade others and thus a definite responsibility to enrich the time to come.

References to Works by J. K. Galbraith Cited in the Text

BOOKS

The Affluent Society (abbreviated to *AS*), revised edition (Harmondsworth: Penguin Books, 1973).

The Age of Uncertainty (London: British Broadcasting Corporation and André Deutsch, 1977).

Ambassador's Journal (London: Hamish Hamilton, 1969).

American Capitalism (abbreviated to *AC*), revised edition (Harmondsworth: Penguin Books, 1967).

The American Left and Some British Comparisons (Fabian Tract 405, 1971).

A China Passage (London: André Deutsch, 1973).

Economic Development (abbreviated to *ED*) (Cambridge: Harvard University Press, 1965).

Economics and the Art of Controversy (abbreviated to *EAC*) (New Brunswick: Rutgers University Press, 1955).

Economics and the Public Purpose (abbreviated to *EPP*) (Harmondsworth: Penguin Books, 1975).

Economics, Peace and Laughter (abbreviated to *EPL*)(Harmondsworth: Penguin Books, 1975).

The Great Crash 1929 (Harmondsworth: Penguin Books, 1969).

How to Control the Military (abbreviated to *HCM*) (Garden City: Doubleday and Company, 1969).

Journey to Poland and Yugoslavia (Cambridge: Harvard University Press, 1958).

The Liberal Hour (abbreviated to *LH*) (Harmondsworth: Penguin Books, 1960).

The McLandress Dimension (written under the pseudonym of Mark Epernay) (London: Hamish Hamilton, 1964).

Made to Last (London: Hamish Hamilton, 1964).

Money: Whence it Came, Where it Went (abbreviated to *Money*) (Harmondsworth: Penguin Books, 1976).

The New Industrial State (abbreviated to *NIS*), revised edition (Harmondsworth: Penguin Books, 1974).

A Theory of Price Control (Cambridge: Harvard University Press, 1952).

The Triumph: A Novel of Modern Diplomacy (London: Hamish Hamilton, 1968).

Who Needs the Democrats (Garden City: Doubleday and Company, 1970). This pamphlet is reprinted in *The American Left, supra*.

ARTICLES

'The Age of the Wordfact', *The Atlantic*, September 1960.

'An Agenda for American Liberals', *Commentary*, June 1966.

'The Big Defense Firms are Really Public Firms and Should be Nationalized', *The New York Times Magazine*, 16 November 1969.

'Buckley v. Vidal, *Esquire*', *National Review*, 13 October 1972.

'The Case for George McGovern', *Saturday Review*, 1 July 1972.

'Countervailing Power', *American Economic Review (Papers and Proceedings)*, 1954.

'The Defense of the Multinational Company', *Harvard Business Review*, March–April 1978.

'Dissent in a Free Society', *The Atlantic*, February 1962.

'The Downing Street Papers', *New Statesman*, 12 December 1975.

'Experiment in India', *Saturday Review*, 15 August 1964.

'Foreign Policy: The Stuck Whistle', *The Atlantic*, February 1965.

'Galbraith Answers Crosland', *New Statesman*, 22 January 1971.

'The Galbraith Plan to Promote the Minorities' (with Edwin Kuh and Lester C. Thurow), *The New York Times Magazine*, 22 August 1971.

'In Defence of N. Krushchev, Author', *New Statesman*, 9 April 1971.

'Inflation: a Presidential Catechism', *The New York Times Magazine*, 15 September 1974.

'Introduction' to T. Veblen, *The Theory of the Leisure Class* (Boston: Houghton Mifflin Company, 1973).

'John Strachey', *Encounter*, September 1963.

'Let Us Begin: an Invitation to Action on Poverty', *Harper's Magazine*, March 1964.

'Market Structure and Stabilization Policy', *Review of Economics and Statistics*, 1957.

'Mr Nixon's Remedy for Inflation', *Harper's Magazine*, February 1960.

'Monopoly and the Concentration of Economic Power', in H. S. Ellis (ed.), *A Survey of Contemporary Economics*, Vol. I (Homewood: Richard D. Irwin, Inc., 1948).

'Perfecting the Corporation: What Comes After General Motors', *The New Republic*, 2 November 1974.

'The Polipollutionists', *The Atlantic*, January 1967.

'The Poor Countries', *Encounter*, October 1953.

'A Positive Approach to Economic Aid', *Foreign Affairs*, April 1961.

'Power and the Useful Economist', *American Economic Review*, 1973.

'The Poverty of Nations', *The Atlantic*, October 1962.

'Professor Gordon on "The Close of the Galbraithian System"', *Journal of Political Economy*, 1969.

'Reflection on the Asian Scene', *Journal of Asian Studies*, August 1964.

'A Review of a Review', *The Public Interest*, Fall 1967.

'Scotland's Greatest Son', *Horizon*, Summer 1974.

'Tasks for the Democratic Left', *The New Republic*, 16 August 1975.

'Tough, Adorable Eleanor', *Sunday Times*, 7 May 1972.

'The Two Voices of America', *Sunday Times*, 4 June 1967.

'United States', *Sunday Times Magazine*, 7 November 1971.

'Wage Controls: Reluctance to Accept the Inevitable', *The Times*, 16 July 1975.

'Will the Answer be Controls?', *The Listener*, 30 January 1975.

'Winning in November is Not Enough', *The New Republic*, 13 June 1970.

Notes

All references are to works by J. K. Galbraith unless otherwise indicated.

1 INTRODUCTION: GALBRAITH AND MARKET CAPITALISM

1. *AS*, p. 35.
2. *EPP*, p. 22.
3. *EPP*, p. 19.
4. *AC*, p. 42.
5. *AS*, p. 14.
6. *NIS*, p. 9.
7. *AS*, p. 248.
8. *EPP*, p. 215.
9. *The Age of Uncertainty*, p. 92.

2 THE TECHNOSTRUCTURE AND ITS GOALS

1. *NIS*, p. 158.
2. *ED*, p. 88.
3. 'The Nature of Social Nostalgia', in *LH*, p. 121.
4. *ED*, p. 88.
5. 'Economics and the Quality of Life', in *EPL*, p. 17.
6. *NIS*, p. 83.
7. *NIS*, p. 83.
8. *NIS*, pp. 179–80.
9. *NIS*, p. 171.
10. *NIS*, p. 108.
11. *NIS*, p. 185.
12. 'Power and the Useful Economist', p. 5.
13. *NIS*, p. 110.
14. *Ambassador's Journal*, p. 13.
15. *EPP*, p. 118.
16. *EPP*, p. 98.
17. *AC*, p. 40.
18. *NIS*, p. 176.
19. *NIS*, p. 170.
20. *NIS*, p. 151.
21. 'Perfecting the Corporation', p. 15.
22. *NIS*, p. 387.
23. *NIS*, p. 94.
24. *EPP*, p. 56.
25. *NIS*, p. 96.

26. 'A Review of a Review', p. 114.
27. *NIS*, p. 386.
28. See 'The Causes of Poverty: a Classification', in *EPL*, pp. 192–3.
29. 'A Differential Prescription', in *EPL*, pp. 202–3.
30. *NIS*, p. 107.
31. *NIS*, pp. 84–5.
32. *NIS*, p. 22.
33. J. Meade, 'Is "The New Industrial State" Inevitable?', *Economic Journal*, 1968, p. 386.
34. R. Marris, '*The New Industrial State*', *The American Economic Review*, 1968, p. 245. In an interview with Myron Sharpe, Galbraith has subsequently made clear that he never intended technical virtuosity to be ranked 'at the same level of importance' as the other two goals enumerated. See 'Conversation with an Inconvenient Economist', in M. Sharpe, *John Kenneth Galbraith and the Lower Economics*, 2nd ed. (White Plains: International Arts and Sciences Press, Inc., 1974), p. 102.
35. *NIS*, p. 127.
36. *NIS*, p. 183.
37. See R. Sheehan, 'Proprietors in the World of Big Business', *Fortune*, 15 June 1967, p. 178.

3 THE TECHNOLOGICAL IMPERATIVE

1. *NIS*, p. 90.
2. *EPP*, p. 62.
3. *AC*, p. 106.
4. *AC*, p. 105.
5. *NIS*, p. 51. See also 'Scotland's Greatest Son' and 'The Defense of the Multinational Company'.
6. *EPP*, pp. 55–6.
7. *NIS*, p. 91.
8. *NIS*, p. 90.
9. *EPP*, p. 132.
10. 'A Review of a Review', p. 113.
11. *NIS*, p. 60.
12. *EPP*, p. 164.
13. *AS*, p. 182.
14. *EAC*, p. 21.
15. *NIS*, p. 269.
16. *NIS*, p. 277.
17. 'A Positive Approach to Economic Aid', p. 447.
18. *ED*, p. 46.
19. *Journey to Poland and Yugoslavia*, p. 61.
20. *NIS*, p. 185.
21. *EPP*, p. 59. Galbraith in *The New Industrial State* refers to the 'planning system' as the 'industrial system'.
22. *Journey to Poland and Yugoslavia*, p. 40.
23. *EPP*, pp. 58–9. The figures refer to 1971.

24. *EPP*, p. 228.
25. 'The Decline of the Machine', in *LH*, p. 38.
26. 'Was Ford a Fraud?', in *LH*, pp. 132–3.
27. Sharpe, op. cit., pp. 13, 14.
28. M. Zinkin, 'Galbraith and Consumer Sovereignty', *Journal of Industrial Economics*, 1967, p. 4.
29. Meade, loc. cit., pp. 377–8.
30. *NIS*, pp. 30n., 211n.
31. Scott Gordon, 'The Close of the Galbraithian System', *Journal of Political Economy*, 1968, p. 639.
32. *EPP*, pp. 155–6.
33. Bob Fitch, 'A Galbraith Reappraisal: the Ideologue as Gadfly', *Ramparts*, 1968; reprinted in E. K. Hunt and J. G. Schwartz (eds.), *A Critique of Economic Theory* (Harmondsworth: Penguin Books, 1972), p. 460.
34. *NIS*, p. 47n.
35. *NIS*, p. 91.
36. See Bruce R. Scott, 'The Industrial State: Old Myths and New Realities', *Harvard Business Review*, 1973.
37. *A Theory of Price Control*, p. 66.
38. *EPP*, p. 204.
39. *NIS*, chs. 23–4.
40. Quoted in 'The Great Mogul', *Time*, 16 February 1968, p. 18.
41. *EPP*, p. 26.
42. 'Market Structure and Stabilization Policy', p. 126.
43. F. McFadzean, *The Economics of John Kenneth Galbraith* (London: Centre for Policy Studies, 1977), p. 10.

4 COUNTERVAILING POWER

1. *AC*, p. 123.
2. *AC*, p. 127.
3. *AC*, p. 129.
4. *AC*, p. 131.
5. *AC*, p. 131.
6. *AC*, p. 132.
7. *AC*, p. 133.
8. *AC*, p. 135.
9. *AC*, p. 155.
10. *AC*, p. 140.
11. 'Countervailing Power', pp. 3–4.
12. 'Power and the Useful Economist', p. 9.
13. *AC*, p. 141.
14. *AC*, p. 181.
15. *AC*, p. 182.
16. *AC*, p. 184.
17. *Ambassador's Journal*, p. 194.
18. 'Countervailing Power', p. 3.
19. *AC*, p. 160.

20. A. Hunter, 'Notes on Countervailing Power', *Economic Journal*, 1958; reprinted in K. W. Rothschild (ed.), *Power in Economics* (Harmondsworth: Penguin Books, 1971), p. 266.
21. Hunter, 'Notes on Countervailing Power', loc. cit., p. 260.
22. *AC*, pp. 128–9.
23. *AC*, p. 164.
24. *Journey to Poland and Yugoslavia*, p. 112.
25. Ibid.
26. *AC*, p. 144.
27. *AC*, p. 146.
28. *AC*, p. 135.
29. *AC*, p. 136.

5 THE SATISFACTION OF WANTS

1. *NIS*, p. 173.
2. *AS*, p. 247.
3. *EPP*, p. 222.
4. *EPP*, p. 157.
5. *NIS*, p. 211.
6. *NIS*, p. 272.
7. 'Tasks for the Democratic Left', p. 19.
8. *NIS*, p. 318.
9. *NIS*, p. 274.
10. 'Economics as a System of Belief', in *EPL*, p. 58n.
11. *EPP*, p. 46.
12. *EPP*, p. 49.
13. *EPP*, p. 52.
14. *EPP*, p. 51.
15. *EPP*, pp. 251–2.
16. *AS*, p. 141.
17. *AS*, p. 141.
18. *AS*, p. 145.
19. *AS*, p. 138.
20. *AS*, p. 140.
21. *NIS*, p. 82.
22. *AS*, p. 143.
23. *NIS*, p. 271.
24. *EPP*, p. 174.
25. *NIS*, p. 323.
26. *AS*, pp. 148–9.
27. *AS*, p. 151.
28. *AS*, p. 154.
29. *AS*, p. 151.
30. *NIS*, p. 218.
31. *NIS*, pp. 273–4.
32. *AS*, p. 152.
33. *NIS*, p. 219.

34. 'Economics as a System of Belief', in *EPL*, pp. 65–6.
35. *NIS*, p. 208.
36. *NIS*, p. 24.
37. *AS*, p. 152.
38. *AC*, p. 110.
39. *AC*, p. 111.
40. 'Economics and the Quality of Life', in *EPL*, p. 19.
41. *AS*, p. 152.
42. J. Strachey, 'Unconventional Wisdom', *Encounter*, October 1958, p. 80. In a tribute to Strachey, Galbraith later returned the compliment: 'If optimism and an open-minded generosity towards the ideas of other people is a vice, it is surely the best of faults. John Strachey was a good and very intelligent man.' ('John Strachey', p. 54).
43. 'The Strategy of Peaceful Competition', in *LH*, p. 22.
44. *NIS*, p. 24.
45. M. Zinkin, 'Galbraith and Consumer Sovereignty', loc. cit., p. 5. See also F. A. von Hayek, 'The *Non Sequitur* of the "Dependence Effect"', *Southern Economic Journal*, 1961; reprinted in Hayek, *Studies in Philosophy, Politics and Economics* (London: Routledge and Kegan Paul, 1967).
46. E. van den Haag, 'Affluence, Galbraith, the Democrats', *Commentary*, 1960, p. 209.
47. 'Economics as a System of Belief', in *EPL*, p. 62.
48. 'The Poor Countries', p. 70.
49. *Made to Last*, p. 31.
50. *Made to Last*, p. 34.
51. *NIS*, p. 371.
52. *NIS*, p. 24. See also 'A Review of a Review', p. 114.
53. *NIS*, p. 122.
54. *ED*, p. 96.
55. *EPP*, pp. 131–2.
56. Scott Gordon, 'The Close of the Galbraithian System', loc. cit., p. 641.
57. 'Professor Gordon on "The Close of the Galbraithian System"', p. 501
58. *NIS*, p. 211.
59. G. C. Allen, *Economic Fact and Fantasy* (London: Institute of Economic Affairs, 1967), p. 20.
60. R. P. Wilder, 'Advertising and Inter-Industry Competition: Testing a Galbraithian Hypothesis', *Journal of Industrial Economics*, 1974, p. 220. Note, however, that books, drugs, soap and detergents are 'exceptional industries which have positive and statistically significant coefficients for absolute advertising', ibid., p. 223.
61. Ibid.
62. *EPP*, 157.
63. *ED*, p. 77.
64. C. A. R. Crosland, 'Production in the Age of Affluence', *The Listener*, 25 September 1958, p. 448. Crosland's essay is reprinted as Chapter 6 of his *The Conservative Enemy* (London: Cape, 1962).
65. It is precisely this stance which enables Galbraith's ideological opponents to accuse him, not entirely unconvincingly, of intolerant paternalism in thinking he knows best what his fellow citizens need. Milton Friedman, for

example, noting that even commercial advertising is a form of free speech, reproaches Galbraith for being a 'tailfin burner' (analogous to the book-burner of an earlier day) and for 'denigrating the tastes of ordinary people, the tastes of those who prefer pushpin to poetry, who prefer large tailfins to nice, compact, expensive little cars'. Friedman goes on to argue that Galbraith deliberately ignores the lack of evidence supporting his hypothesis concerning the machinations of devils who must be disciplined because of a deep-seated missionary zeal to impose his own superior value-system on the community: 'Many reformers—Galbraith is not alone in this—have as their basic objection to a free market that it frustrates them in achieving their reforms, because it enables people to have what they want, not what the reformers want. Hence every reformer has a strong tendency to be adverse to a free market. Galbraith in particular must regard it as trivial or non-existent, or else his whole ideological case, both its justification and its possibility, collapses.' See M. Friedman, *From Galbraith to Economic Freedom* (London: Institute of Economic Affairs, 1977), pp. 14, 32.

6 THE POLITICAL MARKET

  1. *NIS*, p. 372
  2. *EPP*, p. 188.
  3. *EPP*, pp. 158–9.
  4. *EPP*, p. 176.
  5. *EPP*, p. 62.
  6. 'The Big Defense Firms are Really Public Firms and Should be Nationalized', p. 170.
  7. *HCM*, p. 55.
  8. *NIS*, p. 170.
  9. *NIS*, p. 339.
 10. *NIS*, p. 172.
 11. Galbraith has, of course, somewhat modified the implication of mono-causality, as the following random passage indicates: 'None of this is to suggest that all social attitudes originate with the technostructure and its needs. Society also has goals, stemming from the needs which are un-associated with its major productive mechanism, and which it imposes on the mature corporation. As elsewhere I argue only for a two-way process. The mature corporation imposes social attitudes as it also responds to social attitudes. Truth is never strengthened by exaggeration.' (*NIS*, p. 173.) Yet this passage seems to make a mockery of the whole Galbraithian system, appealing as it does to deep-seated social values whose origin and import Galbraith obstinately refuses to make fully explicit. His obsession with the manufactured rather than the authentic causes him never to spell out in detail the nature of the 'two-way process' to which he alludes. And Professor Hession has two further criticisms of the passage under discussion: 'However useful this remark may be from a polemical standpoint, analytically it still leaves us in the dark as to where the balance falls between the two socializing influences. Moreover, Galbraith's qualification implies perhaps that society's goals, derived from its cultural legacy, serve to counteract the attitudes the corporation engenders, when in fact it may be reinforcing them.' C. H.

Hession, *John Kenneth Galbraith and His Critics* (New York: New American Library, 1972), pp. 145–6.
12. *NIS*, p. 174.
13. 'The Big Defense Firms are Really Public Firms and Should Be Nationalized', p. 174.
14. 'Foreign Policy: The Plain Lessons of a Bad Decade', in *EPL*, pp. 144–5.
15. *HCM*, p. 14.
16. 'Foreign Policy: The Plain Lessons of a Bad Decade', in *EPL*, p. 145.
17. 'The American Ambassador', in *EPL*, p. 157.
18. *Who Needs the Democrats*, p. 41.
19. 'John Steinbeck', in *EPL*, p. 260.
20. 'An Agenda for American Liberals', pp. 29–30.
21. *The Triumph*, p. 238.
22. *Who Needs the Democrats*, p. 40.
23. 'The American Ambassador', in *EPL*, p. 159.
24. *The Triumph*, p. 49.
25. *Ambassador's Journal*, p. 187.
26. Ibid., p. 194.
27. Ibid., p. 311.
28. Ibid., p. 374.
29. 'Foreign Policy: The Stuck Whistle', p. 64.
30. 'Foreign Policy: The Plain Lessons of a Bad Decade', in *EPL*, p. 143.
31. Ibid.
32. Ibid.
33. *Ambassador's Journal*, p. 528.
34. Ibid., p. 212.
35. Ibid.
36. Ibid.
37. Ibid.
38. 'Foreign Policy: The Stuck Whistle', p. 65.
39. R. D. Heffner and Esther H. Kramer, 'A Man for All Pursuits', *Saturday Review*, 20 April 1968, p. 35.
40. *HCM*, p. 17.
41. *Who Needs the Democrats*, p. 43.
42. *HCM*, p. 15.
43. *HCM*, p. 16.
44. *HCM*, p. 15.
45. 'The Poverty of Nations', p. 53.
46. *Who Needs the Democrats*, p. 77.
47. 'Power and the Useful Economist', p. 10.
48. *Who Needs the Democrats*, p. 73.
49. *EPP*, p. 260.
50. *The American Left*, p. 29.
51. *Who Needs the Democrats*, p. 49.
52. *EPP*, p. 260.
53. 'Winning in November is Not Enough', p. 14.
54. Ibid.
55. *Who Needs the Democrats*, p. 63.
56. Ibid., p. 44.

57. 'Winning in November is Not Enough', pp. 13–14. In view of Galbraith's graphic use of language, it is no surprise that he is also in favour of relatively loose laws of libel. See 'Buckley v. Vidal, *Esquire*'.
58. *EPP*, pp. 177, 266.
59. *Who Needs the Democrats*, p. 61.
60. *EPP*, p. 319.
61. *HCM*, p. 54.
62. *HCM*, p. 24.
63. *HCM*, p. 54.
64. *The Great Crash*, p. 184.
65. *EPP*, p. 176.
66. *Who Needs the Democrats*, p. 79.
67. 'Dissent in a Free Society', p. 46.
68. *EPP*, p. 337.
69. 'Winning in November is Not Enough', p. 14.
70. *HCM*, p. 53.
71. 'Reflection on the Asian Scene', p. 504.
72. Ibid.
73. Ibid.
74. 'The Polipollutionists', p. 54.
75. 'The Downing Street Papers', p. 758.
76. J. Robinson, '*American Capitalism*', *Economic Journal*, 1952, p. 928.
77. *AC*, p. 165.
78. *NIS*, p. 202.
79. *AC*, p. 189.
80. 'The Big Defense Firms are Really Public Firms and Should be Nationalized', esp. p. 170.
81. *EPP*, p. 303.
82. 'Perfecting the Corporation', p. 16.
83. Ibid., p. 17.
84. See *NIS*, p. 343; *EPP*, pp. 308–9.
85. *EPP*, p. 337.
86. 'The Galbraith Plan to Promote the Minorities', esp. p. 35.
87. See *Money*, 'Mr. Nixon's Remedy for Inflation', "Wage Controls: Reluctance to Accept the Inevitable", "Will the Answer be Controls?", and D. A. Reisman, "Social Justice and Macroeconomic Policy: The Case of J. K. Galbraith", in Aubrey Jones (ed.), *Economics and Equality* (Banbury: Philip Allan, 1976).
88. See 'The Strategy of Peaceful Competition', in *LH*, p. 33; 'Economics as a System of Belief', in *EPL*, p. 66.
89. *EPP*, p. 162.
90. *EPP*, p. 276.
91. *AS*, p. 133. See also 'Galbraith Answers Crosland' and D. A. Reisman, 'Galbraith and Social Welfare', in N. Timms (ed.), *Social Welfare: Why and How?* (London: Routledge and Kegan Paul, 1980).
92. 'William F. Buckley, Jr.: The Unmaking of a Conservative', in *EPL*, p. 250.
93. *Ambassador's Journal*, p. 226.
94. *The Great Crash*, p. 206.
95. 'Richard Nixon', in *EPL*, p. 226.

96. 'The Build-Up and the Public Man', in *LH*, p. 108.
97. Ibid., pp. 109–10.
98. 'Dwight D. Eisenhower, General', in *EPL*, p. 220.
99. *The McLandress Dimension*, pp. 29–30.
100. 'The Age of the Wordfact', pp. 87–8.
101. Ibid., p. 88.
102. Ibid., pp. 88, 90.
103. 'Tough, Adorable Eleanor', p. 16.
104. 'In Defence of N. Krushchev, Author', p. 494.
105. 'United States', p. 97. See also *The Triumph*, p. 88.
106. *The Great Crash*, p. 51.
107. *NIS*, p. 153n.
108. *Ambassador's Journal*, p. 560.
109. *HCM*, p. 16.
110. *The Triumph*, pp. 166–7.
111. *The Great Crash*, p. 51.
112. *NIS*, p. 132.
113. *NIS*, p. 302.
114. *EPP*, p. 266.
115. 'The Age of the Wordfact', p. 90.
116. C. Clark, 'The Horrible Proposals of Mr. Galbraith', *The National Review*, 11 October 1958, p. 237. Colin Clark adds that he finds *The Affluent Society* reminiscent of *1984*.
117. H. Demsetz, 'Where Is The New Industrial State?', *Economic Inquiry*, 1974, p. 12.
118. *EPP*, p. 279.

7 THE EMANCIPATION OF BELIEF

1. *EPP*, p. 247.
2. *EPP*, pp. 247–8.
3. *AS*, p. 230.
4. *NIS*, p. 340.
5. *NIS*, p. 320.
6. *A Theory of Price Control*, p. 4.
7. 'Power and the Useful Economist', p. 10.
8. *NIS*, p. 26.
9. *EPP*, p. 11.
10. *AS*, p. 21.
11. *EAC*, p. 100.
12. *A Theory of Price Control*, p. 4.
13. *EPP*, p. 212.
14. *EPP*, p. 213.
15. 'The Polipollutionists', p. 54.
16. 'United States', p. 99.
17. *EPP*, pp. 309–10.
18. 'Economics as a System of Belief', in *EPL*, p. 65.
19. *EPP*, pp. 43–4.

20. 'Economics as a System of Belief', in *EPL*, p. 65.
21. 'The Build-Up and the Public Man', in *LH*, p. 115.
22. *Made to Last*, p. 125.
23. Ibid., p. 85.
24. *The McLandress Dimension*, p. 93.
25. *EPP*, p. 25.
26. *NIS*, p. 324.
27. 'Economics as a System of Belief', in *EPL*, p. 64.
28. Ibid.
29. 'The Nixon Administration and the Great Socialist Revival', in *EPL*, p. 83.
30. Ibid., pp. 85–6.
31. Ibid., pp. 86–7.
32. 'The Big Defense Firms are Really Public Firms and Should be Nationalized', p. 164.
33. *NIS*, p. 313.
34. 'The Nixon Administration and the Great Socialist Revival', in *EPL*, p. 87.
35. *EPP*, p. 115.
36. 'The Nixon Administration and the Great Socialist Revival', in *EPL*, p. 90.
37. Ibid., p. 91.
38. Ibid., p. 92.
39. Ibid., p. 91.
40. 'Perfecting the Corporation', p. 16.
41. Ibid.
42. *A China Passage*, p. 35.
43. *HCM*, p. 47.
44. *HCM*, pp. 47–8.
45. 'The Case for George McGovern', p. 27.
46. 'United States', p. 93.
47. *HCM*, p. 52.
48. *HCM*, p. 52.
49. *HCM*, p. 52.
50. See, for example, 'The Day Nikita Krushchev Visited the Establishment', in *EPL*, p. 212.
51. *HCM*, p. 43.
52. *The American Left*, p. 30.
53. *HCM*, p. 43.
54. 'Foreign Policy: The Plain Lessons of a Bad Decade', in *EPL*, p. 137.
55. Ibid., p. 141.
56. *HCM*, p. 51.
57. *HCM*, p. 50.
58. 'An Agenda for American Liberals', p. 33.
59. *HCM*, p. 49.
60. 'An Agenda for American Liberals', p. 34.
61. Ibid.
62. *HCM*, p. 49.
63. *NIS*, pp. 364–5.
64. *NIS*, p. 341.
65. *ED*, p. 79.
66. *NIS*, p. 241.

67. *NIS*, p. 369.
68. *NIS*, p. 248.
69. *NIS*, p. 248.
70. *NIS*, p. 249.
71. *AS*, pp. 211–12.
72. *NIS*, p. 364.
73. *NIS*, p. 294.
74. *AS*, p. 228.
75. *ED*, p. 79.
76. *NIS*, p. 367.
77. *NIS*, p. 369.
78. *NIS*, p. 377.
79. *AS*, p. 163.
80. *AS*, p. 163.
81. *NIS*, p. 333.
82. 'United States', p. 99.
83. *NIS*, p. 296.
84. *NIS*, p. 333.
85. Quoted in D. Halberstam, 'The Importance of Being Galbraith', *Harper's Magazine*, November 1967, p. 51.
86. *AC*, p. 44.
87. *NIS*, pp. 374–5.
88. *The American Left*, p. 34.
89. 'Galbraith', interview with Frances Cairncross, *The Observer*, 22 November 1970, p. 25.
90. *NIS*, p. 363.
91. *NIS*, p. 367.
92. 'Reflection on the Asian Scene', p. 503.
93. *ED*, pp. 83–4.
94. *Made to Last*, pp. 132–6.
95. *HCM*, p. 46.
96. *NIS*, p. 359.
97. *NIS*, p. 391.
98. *AS*, p. 278.
99. *Made to Last*, p. 47.
100. *AS*, p. 277.
101. *AS*, p. 276.
102. *AS*, p. 269.
103. *AS*, p. 40.
104. 'Reflection on the Asian Scene', p. 504.
105. See *EPP*, p. 178.
106. 'United States', p. 95.
107. 'Experiment in India', p. 21.
108. 'Galbraith', interview with Frances Cairncross, loc. cit., p. 25.
109. Quoted in Halberstam, 'The Importance of Being Galbraith', loc. cit., p. 50.
110. 'The Great Mogul', *Time*, 16 February 1968, p. 20.
111. See 'The Two Voices of America', p. 10.
112. 'Conversation with an Inconvenient Economist', loc. cit., p. 109.

8 THE VESTED INTEREST

1. *AS*, p. 32.
2. *EPP*, p. 241
3. *AS*, p. 154.
4. 'The Moving Finger Sticks', in *LH*, p. 82.
5. Ibid., p. 90.
6. *AS*, p. 36.
7. *NIS*, p. 331.
8. 'Let Us Begin: An Invitation to Action on Poverty', pp. 16–18.
9. *AC*, p. 24.
10. *AC*, p. 25.
11. *NIS*, p. 175.
12. *NIS*, p. 175.
13. *NIS*, p. 175.
14. *AS*, p. 32.
15. *EPP*, p. 23.
16. 'A Positive Approach to Economic Aid', p. 452.
17. *AS*, p. 34.
18. *EPP*, pp. 342–3.
19. *EPP*, p. 43.
20. *NIS*, p. 220.
21. *EPP*, p. 43.
22. *EPP*, p. 24.
23. 'Economics as a System of Belief', in *EPL*, p. 53.
24. *AS*, p. 31.
25. *AS*, p. 32.
26. *AS*, p. 32.
27. *AS*, p. 31.
28. *AS*, pp. 125–6.
29. *EPP*, p. 342.
30. *AS*, p. 54.
31. *EPP*, p. 24.
32. *EPP*, p. 22.
33. 'Economics as a System of Belief', in *EPL*, p. 53.
34. 'Perfecting the Corporation', p. 14.
35. 'A Positive Approach to Economic Aid', p. 449.
36. 'Power and the Useful Economist', p. 6.
37. *ED*, p. 38.
38. *NIS*, p. 395.
39. 'The Language of Economics', in *EPL*, p. 30; *The Age of Uncertainty*, p. 203.
40. *ED*, p. 38.
41. 'The Language of Economics', in *EPL*, p. 35.
42. *NIS*, pp. 398–9.
43. 'Economics and the Quality of Life', in *EPL*, p. 12.
44. Ibid., pp. 12–13.
45. Ibid., p. 9.
46. 'Power and the Useful Economist', p. 6.
47. *NIS*, p. 393.

48. *ED*, p. 39.
49. *ED*, p. 40.
50. *NIS*, p. 26.
51. 'Power and the Useful Economist', p. 6.
52. 'A Review of a Review', p. 117.
53. *NIS*, p. 376.
54. *NIS*, p. 376.
55. *AS*, p. 140.
56. *AS*, p. 141.
57. 'Economics and the Quality of Life', in *EPL*, p. 13.
58. *NIS*, p. 25.
59. *AS*, p. 244.
60. 'Monopoly and Concentration of Economic Power', p. 103.
61. See C. G. Leathers and J. S. Evans, 'Thorstein Veblen and the New Industrial State', *History of Political Economy*, 1973.
62. *A China Passage*, p. 41.
63. *The Age of Uncertainty*, p. 218.
64. 'Inflation: a Presidential Catechism', p. 14.
65. *NIS*, p. 401.
66. Gordon, 'The Close of the Galbraithian System', loc. cit., p. 636.
67. *NIS*, p. 156.
68. R. Solow, 'Son of Affluence', *The Public Interest*, Fall 1967, pp. 100–1.
69. Ibid., p. 101.
70. P. A. Samuelson, 'Galbraith', *Newsweek*, 3 July 1967, p. 53.
71. C. Bliss, 'Galbraith on the New Capitalism', *New Blackfriars*, 1968, p. 312.
72. *NIS*, p. 323.
73. *EPP*, p. 161.
74. 'Introduction' to *The Theory of the Leisure Class*, p. xiv.
75. H. G. Johnson, 'A Modern Tawney', *The Spectator*, 19 September 1958, p. 381.

9 CONCLUSION: GALBRAITH AND THE EMANCIPATION OF BELIEF

1. 'Dissent in a Free Society', p. 45.
2. Ibid., p. 46.
3. Halberstam, 'The Importance of Being Galbraith', loc. cit., p. 52.
4. See 'The Great Mogul', *Time*, 16 February 1968, p. 18.
5. 'The Case for George McGovern', p. 27.
6. Ibid., p. 24.
7. Ibid.
8. Ibid., p. 27.
9. Ibid., p. 26.
10. *EPP*, p. 261.
11. 'Critic of Affluence', *The Listener*, 6 May 1965, p. 657.
12. 'Reflection on the Asian Scene', p. 503.
13. Heffner and Kramer, 'A Man for All Pursuits', loc. cit., p. 36.
14. 'Galbraith's Republic', *The Economist*, 9 September 1967, p. 894.
15. Halberstam, 'The Importance of Being Galbraith', loc. cit., p. 48.

16. Ibid., p. 50.
17. 'Author at Home', *Newsweek*, 8 August 1960, p. 58.
18. *NIS*, p. 12.
19. *Ambassador's Journal*, p. 589.
20. Ibid., p. 594.

Index